MW00399865

BroadStreet Publishing® Group, LLC
Savage, Minnesota, USA
BroadStreetPublishing.com

Engaging Heaven Today for Women: 365 Daily Devotions
Copyright © 2022 James Levesque

978-1-4245-6274-9 (faux leather)
978-1-4245-6275-6 (ebook)

For custom editions of BroadStreet Publishing titles may be purchased
for educational, business, ministry, fundraising, or sales promotional
information, please email orders@broadstreetpublishing.com.

Cover and interior by Garborg Design Works | garborgdesign.com

Printed in China

22 23 24 25 26 5 4 3 2 1

ENGAGING

HEAVEN

TODAY

FOR WOM

365 Daily Dev

BroadStre
PUBLISHING

Dedication

I want to dedicate this devotional to the greatest woman of God I know: my bride, Debbie. Thank you for loving Jesus and our family and for living out the devotions in this book. We created this together.

January

Knowing God's Faithfulness

Through the LORD's mercies we are not consumed,
Because His compassions fail not.
They are new every morning;
Great is Your faithfulness.
LAMENTATIONS 3:22–23 NKJV

People are unreliable. They break their promises, kick you when you're down, and judge you if you're struggling. But have you ever had a friend who was so faithful you knew you could count on them no matter what? They love you, point you back toward God, and are always there to help you. They go the extra mile. Friends like that are such a blessing, and nobody is more like that kind of friend than Jesus. Nobody is more faithful and loyal than he. He is willing to meet you wherever you are and go as far as is needed to help you. He is more reliable than the sun. So, whatever you're believing for in this new year, maintain a framework of faithfulness by trusting that God is going to be there for you no matter what comes your way. You are not alone. You are *never* alone. He is your closest friend and will never let you down.

ENGAGING HEAVEN

As you make plans for this new year, have you invited Jesus on your journey?

Things of Old

"Do not remember the former things,
Nor consider the things of old."

Isaiah 43:18 NKJV

Are you ready for this new year? Are you ready to forget the former things and press on toward the new things God is doing in your life? Are you ready to let go of your past hurts and failures and move on? There are people in your life who have hurt you. Do those offenses still hold you back, or are you willing to forgive them even if those who hurt you never ask you for forgiveness? Perhaps you are struggling to let go of damaging relationships. Consider that they may be holding you back from new relationships the Lord wants to bless you with. Are you willing to let go and trust God so you may find healing and blessing? We can't be wise without the wisdom of God. As we become wise, it is pertinent that we embrace the new things God is bringing us to. He is always doing new things, and he gives us grace to receive what he is releasing; however, it's often through the door of forgetting the things of old.

ENGAGING HEAVEN

What in your past is holding you back?

Blind Leading the Blind

He spoke a parable to them:
"Can the blind lead the blind?
Will they not both fall into the ditch?"
LUKE 6:39 NKJV

When are you going to stop going to Negative Nancy's home group? Or listening to Doubting Donna? You may not realize it right away, but people either pull you to greatness or reduce you to unbelief. Don't ask directions from people who are not at the place you are trying to reach. Don't take advice from the lost or the blind. You cannot allow people's disapproval or approval to control you. You are not an orphan running around, trying to win approval from people. The approval you need is from your Father in heaven. It is from his approval alone that your heart will truly feel full. Stop worrying about being misunderstood and start desiring to please God alone. When you seek first God's kingdom, people will no longer be able to tear you down because you're standing on ground that cannot be moved.

ENGAGING HEAVEN

Who are the people in your life pushing you closer toward God and spurring you on to greatness?

Peace and Wisdom

Her teachings are filled with wisdom and kindness
as loving instruction pours from her lips.

PROVERBS 31:26 TPT

Peace is an invaluable aid for decision-making. Peace guides our hearts in the right direction. If a decision doesn't bring us peace, it's a good indication that we probably shouldn't follow through with it. A lack of peace is the Lord's way of checking you, maybe giving you a nudge that something is not right. Colossians 3:15 takes peace one step further by instructing, "Let the peace of God rule in your hearts, to which also you were called in one body; and be thankful" (NKJV). We don't make decisions by ourselves because we are part of a bigger body. People who isolate themselves have a broken decision maker, which inevitably leads to a lack of peace. We need prayer and we need people in order to find peace. So, let's make sure we are on our knees in prayer regularly and that we surround ourselves with wise and reliable people. That way, when those defining moments in life come, we will be able to make good decisions and lead a peaceful life.

ENGAGING HEAVEN

Is there a decision you need to make today that is stealing your peace? Pray and ask God to give you peace in your situation.

Daily Bread

"Give us this day
our daily bread."
MATTHEW 6:11 NKJV

Jesus had just finished explaining how God provides for us so we don't need to worry, and then he follows it by saying, "Seek first the kingdom of God and His righteousness, and all these things shall be added to you" (v. 33). What things? Everything. Everything we worry about, everything we strive for, everything we need. He continues by instructing us to "not worry about tomorrow, for tomorrow will worry about its own things. Sufficient for the day is its own trouble" (v. 34). Every day God offers us spiritual manna from heaven, food for our souls. He's a loving God who is always there for us, but if we don't live according to his principles, we won't acquire our desired results. He's number one, and there is no number two. He is our everything. Everything we do, everything we are, everything we have is given to us through the filter of serving God.

ENGAGING HEAVEN

What are you focusing on today that is stealing your joy for tomorrow? What can you focus on today that will give you peace for tomorrow?

Find Your Jericho

"Are you weary, carrying a heavy burden?
Come to me. I will refresh your life,
for I am your oasis."
MATTHEW 11:28 TPT

David had a friend named Nahash, who was king of the Ammonites. When Nahash died, David sent two men as dignitaries to pay condolences. The Ammonites doubted David's intentions and thought the men had come to spy, so instead of receiving the two men, they cut off their beards and the back of their pants so their backsides were exposed. Humiliated, the men returned to David discouraged, upset, and afraid. David stopped them before they entered the city. Instead of bringing them back to be embarrassed in front of their own people, he sent them to Jericho where they could stay, regain their strength, grow their beards back, and find rest. Then David went and overthrew the Ammonites (2 Samuel 10). Has life treated you unfairly? Have you been humiliated and brought low? God says that vengeance is his and that he is the one who will repay (Romans 12:19). And, honestly, he will do a much better job of it than you. So, go find your Jericho, regain your strength, and trust your King to defend you.

ENGAGING HEAVEN

Are you weary and discouraged? Go to the Lord for strength and encouragement. Trust him to fight your battles.

In His Image

Then God said,
"Let Us make man in Our image,
according to Our likeness."
GENESIS 1:26 NKJV

God's plan from the beginning was to create us in his image.
The greatest tragedy today is that we are spending all our
time trying to recreate God in our image. We need to stop
attempting to pull the Lord down to our level. When Romans
12:2 (NKJV) tells us, "Do not be conformed to this world,"
the word used for "world" is *ion*, which means "a period of
time." In our modern age, we could say, "Stop trying to fit in
with today's dead church culture." Why is the measuring stick
for our future the lack we've seen in the past? Today, dream
again. today, separate yourself to God. Stop trying so hard.
Stop everything you're planning on doing and just spend
time with the Lord today. Don't waste all your energy trying
to please other people when the only one whose opinion of
you really matters is your Father. Seek to please him.

ENGAGING HEAVEN

*You were created to bear God's image. Are you being true
and faithful to that in the way you live your life?*

No Means No

We must be so full of integrity
that our "Yes" or "No" is convincing enough
and we do not stumble into hypocrisy.
JAMES 5:12 TPT

Some people really struggle to say no to requests from others. Because of this, they have a myriad of relationship issues and boundary issues. The word *no* is one of the most powerful words because it can save relationships by establishing healthy boundaries. We need to learn how to use it; otherwise, we will end up as frustrated, overworked doormats. "No" is powerful. It is equipping. It is empowering both for us and for others because by setting personal parameters, we allow and encourage other people to do what we really can't do right now. Refusing to set those parameters by agreeing to every request asked of us will cost us our relationships and leave us burned out. In our effort to please everyone, we're losing our ability to have relationships. Real relationships will, in time, require conflicting and confronting conversations. These aren't a bad thing. They're a healthy part of life. It's so important to learn how to say, "I can't do this. I'm sorry. The answer is no."

ENGAGING HEAVEN

Are you prepared to protect yourself, your time with God, your family, and your relationships by occasionally disappointing people?

On-the-Job Training

He arose and rebuked the wind,
and said to the sea, "Peace, be still!"
And the wind ceased and there was a great calm.
But He said to them, "Why are you so fearful?
How is it that you have no faith?"
MARK 4:39–40 NKJV

The disciples got into a boat, and the Bible says, regarding Jesus, "They took Him along in the boat *as He was*" (v. 36, emphasis added). Whoever Jesus was in your life three weeks ago is who he is today. Circumstances may change, the weather certainly will change, but he won't change. If you did not believe that he was your provider, you didn't trust him with your finances, then how are you going to trust him now in the middle of a storm? This is not on-the-job training; you've been on the job this entire time. When it comes to faith, the worst time to learn is in crisis. Is it possible? Yes. Is God with you? Absolutely. Is grace available? There's no doubt about it. But the best time to learn isn't during a storm, because if you had doubts when everything was calm, why would you trust him now that the waves are crashing down?

ENGAGING HEAVEN

Today is the day to turn off the television and spend time with Jesus. Tomorrow may be a storm. How can you know? You can only prepare.

Pray for Your Authority

Pray for every political leader and representative,
so that we would be able to live tranquil, undisturbed lives,
as we worship the awe-inspiring God with pure hearts.

1 TIMOTHY 2:2 TPT

What Paul said about praying for authority is fascinating because, at this time, Nero was king. He was known for burning and killing thousands of Christians. And yet, in this era when people were terrified of the emperor and hated him, Paul said to pray for him. See, something happens in our hearts when we pray for those who are in authority. Something releases in us when we choose to respect and love those in authority instead of fearing and hating them. For starters, we cannot live in peace if we're not praying for those in authority over us. So, it doesn't matter who the president is and whether it's the candidate you voted for or not, we need to pray for the president. Whoever your boss or teacher or governor is, pray. It's time we put down our flesh, get outside of how we feel, and pray for them.

ENGAGING HEAVEN

Who in authority will you pray for today?

Preparing for Storms

The Lord is good,
A stronghold in the day of trouble;
And He knows those who trust in Him.

NAHUM 1:7 NKJV

Fear is not the issue. Every person on the planet will feel fearful from time to time. What matters is what we do in the face of fear. Does faith or fear dictate our decisions? The enemy uses fear to try to manipulate us and steal away our destiny. For some people, when a storm is brewing, it's terrifying because fear controls them. For others, it's exhilarating because they are filled with faith, and they know God is up to something. There is no condemnation if we don't feel ready for the storm. However, God equips us. Those who have prepared, live ready, and already have faith in their hearts will undoubtedly fare better amid life's storms.

ENGAGING HEAVEN

*Do you see the storms of life as frightening
or as opportunities?*

Salvation Swap

"O My Father, if it is possible,
let this cup pass from Me;
nevertheless, not as I will, but as You will."
MATTHEW 26:39 NKJV

The Old Testament points to the New Testament in a perfectly symbiotic way. In the Old Testament, salvation was often referred to as a "cup." David poetically depicted that his "cup runs over" (Psalm 23:5 NKJV). But then in the New Testament, Jesus came along and said to the woman at the well, "Whoever drinks of this water will thirst again, but whoever drinks of the water that I shall give him will never thirst. But the water that I shall give him will become in him a fountain of water springing up into everlasting life" (John 4:13–14 NKJV). Jesus took a cup and made it into a well; not just any well but a well springing up *inside* us! A cup of salvation in the Old Testament, a well of salvation in the New Testament. The difference was Jesus. In the Old Testament, our suffering was a well, and we were constantly digging and drawing. Our salvation was a cup. But because Jesus came, our trials are now nothing more than a cup, but we have his well of blessing always inside us.

ENGAGING HEAVEN

Do you want a cup or a well? It's time to throw your cup down and prepare to receive the full well of salvation and blessing.

She Shall Not Be Moved

God is in the midst of her,
she shall not be moved;
God shall help her,
just at the break of dawn.

PSALM 46:5 NKJV

Think about the things you're frustrated with today. Think about the things you haven't received answers for. Maybe you're praying for more finances, peace in your marriage, or joy in your home. Maybe you need a miracle in your body. Do you have unending hope over it? Are you confessing the Scriptures? Are you believing for the best? Romans 4:18 tells us that Abraham, "contrary to hope, in hope believed" (NKJV). In other words, even though there was no possible way, he trusted God. He wasn't earthly wishing...he was heavenly hoping. He had absolute anticipation that God was going to move on his behalf, and we can have that confidence too. As Christians, we have to start believing in miracles again. We have to be a people with contagious hope. We don't need doomsday prophets. What we need are prophets of hope and deliverance, rising up, declaring the Word of the Lord, and believing that God can do anything.

ENGAGING HEAVEN

If Christians do nothing or look like the world, how will the world get any better? How are you living differently than the world? In what ways do you look like Jesus?

Take the Baby

"So likewise, whoever of you
does not forsake all that he has
cannot be My disciple."
LUKE 14:33 NKJV

First Kings 3 tells the story of two harlots who both gave birth to sons. One of the babies died, and both mothers claimed the living baby was theirs. So, King Solomon ordered the living baby to be chopped in half and one half given to each mother. Of course, the true mother immediately insisted that the other woman could have the baby and just asked that he not be killed. Solomon immediately restored her son back to her because it was evident that she was the real mother. There will be times when you feel the need to defend what is yours and someone else will try to steal it or destroy it. In your life, that baby may symbolize your reputation, ministry, success, or even your heart. Maybe they want to tear down what you have created and love. Be willing to release it to God and watch him give it right back to you. If he established it and birthed it through you, then he's the only one who can restore and preserve it.

ENGAGING HEAVEN

*What is the "baby" in your life that you have worked
so hard to create?*

When Life Goes Wrong

Before you judge the wickedness of others,
you had better remember this: you are also without excuse,
for you too are guilty of the same kind of things!
ROMANS 2:1 TPT

Why does God receive all the blame when things go wrong?
The darkness in this world has a lot to do with us failing to
follow Jesus and do what he told us to do. We're on this
earth to point to Jesus, to offer this world light and hope
and a better way. Instead, we're constantly fighting our flesh,
criticizing, and casting judgment. It takes zero anointing to
sit at home and declare God's judgment. When things go
horribly in life, it may be because we're doing something
right and the devil is opposing us, or we're doing something
wrong and suffering the natural consequences of our own
poor decisions. Why do we assume every storm was sent by
an angry God? If that was God's way of sending judgment,
then when Jesus rebuked the storm (Mark 4:39), he was
basically rebuking his own action. Jesus rebuked the storms
and commanded the waves. That's your job now.

ENGAGING HEAVEN

*When things go wrong in your life, what is your first
assumption?*

A Future of Hope

For I know the thoughts that I think toward you,
    says the LORD,
thoughts of peace and not evil,
to give you a future and a hope.

JEREMIAH 29:11 NKJV

When the Father came to Jeremiah assuring him of a future and a hope, Jeremiah was twenty years into a fifty-year exile. He still had thirty years to go. We love the Lord's promises, but we don't like waiting for them. In today's culture, our patience is at an all-time low, and so is our hope. Lack of hope is leading to a lack of miracles, power, and belief. We allow the disappointments of life to overtake us. One man hurt you and now "all men are dogs." Someone took advantage of your generosity and suddenly "everyone is out to get me." The devil wants to shape your world through unbelief, anger, and hopelessness so that you never dream with God or see breakthrough. But it's a lie. Your future isn't bleak...it's filled with promise and hope. It's time to dream with God again because one of the most powerful realms of heaven is available for those willing to hope.

ENGAGING HEAVEN

Can you imagine being twenty years into a fifty-year prison sentence when the Lord promises that your future is filled with hope and peace?

Implantation of Faith

So then faith comes by hearing,
and hearing by the word of God.
ROMANS 10:17 NKJV

The plan of God is pretty simple: he gives us the implantation of faith, and we cultivate the atmosphere to see it grow. The power is not in our efforts, but it's in his Word. It's not your abilities; it is God who creates the growth. But you will not birth the promises of God unless you follow Christ...*actually* follow him. We have to be moved to action by what the Word of God says and what the Lord has spoken to us. The power of God, his presence, and what he paid for on the cross are everything to us. But we have to stop looking at this crooked earth and corrupt Christian era for some kind of response. It may not be by your timeline, it may seem frustrating, you may have up and downs, but the bottom line is that God does not change.

ENGAGING HEAVEN

Start giving praise and glory and thanks to God and watch your life turn around.

Power of Integrity

He who walks with integrity walks securely,
But he who perverts his ways will become known.
PROVERBS 10:9 NKJV

Integrity is important and is found in who we are when
nobody else is there. If we always tell the truth, we'll never
have to cover up a lie. People are watching us, and they need
examples. Compromisers don't reach people. There's power
in conviction because conviction holds us accountable.
Conviction leads to integrity and godliness and standing
for what we believe in. Many times, we don't think people
are paying attention, but they are. They're noticing, and this
includes our children. If we think we're hiding our sin and
keeping it a secret, it'll burn us from the inside out. Who are
you in the dark at your core when there are no apparent
consequences? Would you put everything you do online in
front of the congregation to see on Sunday morning? Live
so that who you are in the dark is the same person you are
during the daylight. Allow God to transform your life and
then be a true example of integrity.

ENGAGING HEAVEN

*People want to know if you're the real deal, if you're truly a
woman of integrity.*

Social Media Mayhem

Be faithful to pray as intercessors
who are fully alert and giving thanks to God.
COLOSSIANS 4:2 TPT

God deserves the glory. Whether it's trendy or not, it's not okay to glory in pain or broadcast our trials for the sake of drawing attention. God is at work, and the spotlight should be on him. It is far more beneficial to share our struggles with a few close friends for prayer instead of making new social media posts every time life gets difficult. Paul wrote at length about all the struggles he was constantly enduring, but he always concluded with assigning the glory where it was due: to God. He wrote, "So I'm not defeated by my weakness, but delighted! For when I feel my weakness and endure mistreatment—when I'm surrounded with troubles on every side and face persecution because of my love for Christ—I am made yet stronger. For my weakness becomes a portal to God's power" (2 Corinthians 12:10 TPT). The devil wants us to fantasize and publicize the heartache, but in truth, our weaknesses invite God's power to work, and *that* should be the focus of our attention.

ENGAGING HEAVEN

What is the purpose of your social media posts? Are they so you can garner pity and attention, or are they to celebrate God's victory through the trials?

Training Wheels

O God, You have taught me from my youth;
And to this day I declare Your wonderous works.
PSALM 71:17 NKJV

Have you ever noticed that when people become new
believers, it seems like no matter what they do, it is blessed?
They pray for somebody, and God touches that person.
They tithe, and God multiplies it. Well, that is because God
is teaching and training them for greatness. It's like training
wheels on a bike. In time, however, the training wheels come
off, and we wipe out a little more often. This could come in
the form of a good friend or someone you really counted on
no longer being there. Maybe it came as a job change or loss.
Whatever it was that got shaken in your life, it's not all loss.
Many times, God is just removing your training wheels so you
can ride even faster and farther. He's calling you to reach new
heights. For a moment you feel out of control and scared,
and perhaps you fall down a time or two, but before you
know it, you're soaring.

ENGAGING HEAVEN

*You can't do what God is calling you to do at your current
level of comfort. You can't do great things for heaven
without being stretched.*

Who Are You?

In Him dwells all the fullness
of the Godhead bodily;
and you are complete in Him.
COLOSSIANS 2:9–10 NKJV

Who are you? How you see yourself is indicative of who you'll become. People who view themselves as not good enough or an inconvenience to others in time realize the self-fulfilling prophesy they cursed themselves with. That's who they become, apologetically saying things like, "I don't want to bother you" or "I know you're busy." They don't want to inconvenience anyone in their life because they *believe* they are an inconvenience. Have you ever thought that perhaps you're a blessing to be around? Has it occurred to you that maybe people like helping and look forward to when you come around? But if you live with this rejection mentality, you throw that on everybody else and assume they reject you, too, at least in their hearts. Evaluate who you are, where you are in life, and make it count.

ENGAGING HEAVEN

Who are you when you're not defining yourself by your responsibilities?

Defining the Difficult

All discipline seems to be painful at the time,
yet later it will produce a transformation of character,
bringing a harvest of righteousness and peace
to those who yield to it.

HEBREWS 12:11 TPT

Yes, God disciplines those he loves, but discipline is
not judgment. There's a difference between discipline,
persecution, suffering, and judgment. God could do anything
he wants to do. His nature is to overcome and to heal, to
set free and to save. But there is also a devil on the loose in
this world. Persecution is something every believer will face
because we have an enemy who hates the one we serve.
That's persecution for righteousness' sake, like what Job
underwent. The problem is that whenever anything hard
happens, everybody thinks they're just like Job. However,
sometimes we're just suffering because of the broken state
of the world. Suffering happens to everyone. When we lay
hands on the sick, why would we assume it was God who
put that sickness in them? It might not have been God who
caused that mom to miscarry...it could have been the devil or
the terrible condition of the world we live in. Judgment will
come one day, and it will be much stronger in the house of
God. But that is not what we're witnessing today.

ENGAGING HEAVEN

*How can you tell if you're being disciplined because
the Father loves you or if you're being persecuted
because the devil hates you?*

Let Your Light Shine

"I have destined you to become
a beacon light for the nations
and release salvation to the ends of the earth!"
Acts 13:47 TPT

When a light is plugged in, it shines. Similarly, we are only going to be effective if we are plugged into God and his Word. If we're running around on low battery, our light is not going to shine bright. We live in a day of fabrication, but we can't fake light. You can grow in favor, and you can absolutely grow out of favor. There have been mighty people who let their lights go out and fell out of favor because they weren't spending time with the Lord. If we want power publicly, it starts with being grounded privately because God is our source of power. Desire alone is not enough. Many people have built great lamp stands, but they have no light. If we're not connected to the Holy Spirit, we're not going to shine no matter how hard we try. The desire of God is that Jesus Christ would live inside of us and that the light of Christ would shine through. That is why we're on this earth.

ENGAGING HEAVEN

Are you plugged in?
Are you connected to the power source?

Perilous Times

Whatever things were written before
were written for our learning,
that we through the patience and comfort
of the Scriptures might have hope.

ROMANS 15:4 NKJV

People are always looking for an escape. When the world around us reflects the end times, it's time to get focused. The Bible tells us it will be a "great and dreadful day" (Malachi 4:5 NKJV). Do not believe for a second that we have no hope. This is neither the best nor the worst that it's going to be. Habakkuk 2:14 says, "The earth will be filled with the knowledge of the glory of the LORD, as the waters cover the sea" (NKJV). Perhaps these are perilous times, but God has put you where you are supposed to be for right now. How are you maximizing what God is giving you? We are going to see a mighty harvest come into the kingdom, but there is going to be a separation. You're going to be given what you want. If you want Christ, he will come to you. If you want the things of the flesh, that's what you'll receive. Whom are you serving?

ENGAGING HEAVEN

We're in perilous times. What are you going to do about it?

Sarah Considered

Consider the work of God;
For who can make straight
what He has made crooked?
ECCLESIASTES 7:13 NKJV

Abraham and Sarah have been given a promise that they will have a child, yet they're both well into their senior years. Still, the Lord confirmed to Abraham, "Sarah your wife shall have a son" (Genesis 18:10 NKJV). Well, Sarah was listening and laughed at the Lord. When he confronted her on it, she denied it because she was scared. It's never a good idea to mock God, right? Fast-forward to Hebrews 11:11, which says, "By faith Sarah herself also received strength to conceive seed, and she bore a child when she was past the age, because she judged Him faithful who had promised" (NKJV). Wasn't this the same Sarah who laughed at God? Now the verse is referring to her as "faithful"? See, God doesn't hold you to your past confusion. The destiny that God has called you to is directly connected to you considering him faithful. It may take you some time to come to terms with the incredible way he does things, but he is patient. God works through surrendered individuals, even if it takes them a bit of time to catch up.

ENGAGING HEAVEN

You are pregnant with promises, and you have a major part to play in birthing them and fulfilling them in your life.

The Beauty of Vulnerability

> "Judge not, that you be not judged.
> For with what judgment you judge,
> you will be judged;
> and with the measure you use,
> it will be measured back to you."
>
> MATTHEW 7:1–2 NKJV

Always consider the best in someone, not the worst. If you're trying to shine light on other people's weaknesses while your own life is in darkness, it isn't going to end well for you. When you start looking critically at someone, there's almost no hope left for you to learn and grow because everything you think and see will be through a critical lens. If you are harboring hurt and offense, that's a problem that will steal your peace, joy, and love. Ultimately, it's a lack of trust in God because that's where you should be finding your worth, not in what other people say. When you focus on Jesus and choose to love, hurt and offense no longer hold any power over you. When you're vulnerable before the Lord and allow him to clean out your heart of all the worldly nastiness that found its way in there, then you bring it all to light and no longer live in darkness. Suddenly, you live in freedom, and nothing can break you down.

ENGAGING HEAVEN

Have you embraced the beauty of vulnerability, or are you hiding things in your heart that don't belong there?

True Beauty

Let your true beauty come from your inner personality,
not a focus on the external.
For lasting beauty comes from a gentle and peaceful spirit,
which is precious in God's sight and is much more important
than the outward adornment of elaborate hair, jewelry, and
fine clothes.
1 PETER 3:3–4 TPT

God does not want you to suffer. But we suffer through
things for righteousness' sake. If we are truly standing for
Christ, then we will deal with persecution. It's not bad; it's
actually natural. Not everything uncomfortable is an attack
from the enemy. We're sharing in the suffering of Christ
just like we will one day share in his inheritance. If there's
nothing in your life worth persecuting, you may be stuck in
a comfortable middle ground that doesn't bear any fruit.
God wants you filled with faith and boldness, which is true
beauty. As long as Jesus is shining through you, you'll be full
of peace and love, bearing fruit, and leaving a lasting impact.
Leave your mark on this world; don't let this world leave its
mark on you. You're beautiful, truly, so let your light shine and
stay that way.

ENGAGING HEAVEN

*Many people lose their beauty when they allow life to
discourage them and make them cynical. Are you holding on
to your sweetness? Do you still forgive? Do you see the best
in others? Are you truly beautiful?*

Viper Eggs

They hatch vipers' eggs and weave the spider's web;
He who eats of their eggs dies,
And from that which is crushed a viper breaks out.

ISAIAH 59:5 NKJV

Isaiah warned that these snake eggs were hatching in their minds, and they were becoming entangled in spider webs. By succumbing to today's "anything goes" watered-down version of Christianity and welcoming the world's ways into our lives, our minds can easily become poisoned, and we can fall into snares. There's a web of addiction. There's a web of no rules. There are so many webs. We were not meant to live with patterns of sin or to live dishonestly. Sure, we can get away with a few hidden sins, but ultimately, it's a sticky trap that will come back and bite us. We've got to be a little more on guard because sin starts small. We probably won't wake up one morning with murderous thoughts, but we will be tempted to try to cover our last lie or act manipulatively. It may seem small and insignificant, but our iniquity will poison our minds and leave us ensnared.

ENGAGING HEAVEN

By your choices, you build habits of either faith or unbelief. Being close to the Lord matters, purity matters, and limiting the number of voices speaking into your life matters. Guard your heart so you don't become ensnared.

Christian Rollercoaster

You were called to live this way,
because Christ also suffered in your place,
leaving you his example for you to follow.

1 Peter 2:21 TPT

Luke 9:57–58 tells this story: "Now it happened as they journeyed on the road, that someone said to Him, 'Lord, I will follow You wherever You go.' And Jesus said to him, 'Foxes have holes and birds of the air have nests, but the Son of Man has nowhere to lay His head'" (NKJV). Whoever made this declaration was most likely sincere, but he probably didn't fully understand what he was volunteering for. Not only was Jesus homeless at the time, but he was traveling south of Galilee to Jerusalem where he would ultimately be crucified while his friends scattered, terrified. At the time, Jesus was preaching, performing miracles, and doing all sorts of amazing things that would make following him seem appealing. But soon he would be killed. That's the rollercoaster of following Jesus. If we're truly committed to being his disciples, we need to live with the resolve of knowing that both good and bad are coming our way, but no matter what, God is going to provide. That's why faith is so important.

ENGAGING HEAVEN

Consider your social media accounts. Are you prepared to follow Christ through the good times and the bad?

Mystery

"Can you search out the deep things of God?
Can you find out the limits of the Almighty?"

JOB 11:7 NKJV

Faith thrives in the realm of mystery. To do great things for God many times will require you to stand in places of unknowing. That's a beautiful place to be. There's a dependence on God required that will result in the blooming of faith. We may lose loved ones or face bitter disappointment, and we may not initially understand why. While that's hard, it would be a lot harder if we weren't living in the realm of faith. There are some things we just can't reconcile, but faith thrives in the place of trust. As long as we're determined to control the narrative of our lives, we cannot experience the depth of relationship God wants to share with us. We will never live the abundant life or see all that God has planned if we cannot learn to let everything else go and cling to trusting the character of Christ.

ENGAGING HEAVEN

What do you need to release control of?

Delight

Delight yourself also in the Lord,
And He shall give you the desires of your heart.
Psalm 37:4 NKJV

The Lord is delightful! Know him, make him known, pray to him, worship him, receive his love, receive the presence of God in your life, delight in him. The Bible says God will give you the desires of your heart. It doesn't say if you go to a worship service, he'll give you a Lexus. What it's actually saying is that when you delight yourself in the Lord, when you make him your all in all, when you step into the beauty of who he is, he will give you what you desire because your desires will change. The things you want to do will change. What is important to you is going to change. The goals and visions you have for your life, your family, and your job are all going to change. They'll become God's desires. Your dreams will become God's dreams. God wants to increase your awareness of him and fulfill your deepest desires.

ENGAGING HEAVEN

Identity releases destiny. When you know who you are, when you're secure in who God has made you to be, your destiny will come forth.

February

One Day

"Every man at the beginning sets out the good wine,
and when the guests have well drunk, then the inferior.
You have kept the good wine until now!"

JOHN 2:10 NKJV

When Jesus was at a wedding feast, he turned water to wine.
The wine was so good that the master of the feast observed
that the bridegroom had saved the best wine for last. This
is a worthwhile metaphor for life because believing that the
best wine is served last is like believing we're living every
day for another time down the road. So many believers
live for "one day" in the future. One day they'll experience
breakthrough, one day they'll lose weight, one day they'll go
back to school. But "one day" never comes, friends. The best
season of life is now. *Now* is where God has us and when
we should be living. Don't give all your energy and hope to
someday down the road. Faith is today. See, he's not a God
of someday. He's the God of here and now. The best wine
isn't served last. It's served now.

ENGAGING HEAVEN

How is God working in your life today?

Secret Place

When you pray, go into your room,
and when you have shut your door,
pray to your Father who is in the secret place;
and your Father who sees in secret
will reward you openly.

MATTHEW 6:6 NKJV

Do you ever wonder where God is? Well, he is in the secret place where he wants to meet you. Jesus knew the importance of meeting with God, and he demonstrated this for us. He woke up in the morning before the sun had risen, and "He went out and departed to a solitary place; and there He prayed" (Mark 1:35 NKJV). Even the disciples were so busy doing ministry that they barely had time to eat, so Jesus called to them and said, "Come aside by yourselves to a deserted place and rest a while" (Mark 6:31 NKJV). The question is: Are you going to meet God in his secret place, or are you distracted on your phone? A phone is a great tool when it's used in moderation and put in its proper place, but it seems so much easier to post than to pray. The Bible warns us that "the desires for other things entering in choke the word, and it becomes unfruitful" (Mark 4:19 NKJV). If you are under the power of that distraction, it's going to hurt your heart and your relationship with God.

ENGAGING HEAVEN

Go somewhere alone to spend time with God and don't bring your phone.

The Rosetta Stone

"He who received seed on the good ground
is he who hears the word and understands it."
MATTHEW 13:23 NKJV

The Rosetta stone was an actual stone found by a French soldier named Pierre Bouchard in 1799. He was stationed in Egypt at Fort Julien in Rosetta. One day while doing his rounds, Bouchard came across writing on a stone. What was etched there was a trilingual text, given in Greek and two different kinds of ancient Egyptian. This key enabled people to translate hieroglyphics. The Rosetta stone ended up being the standard for a whole language. When Jesus told the parable of the farmer who sowed seeds, he said that this parable was the one against which every other parable would be measured. If we couldn't understand this one, he said, we wouldn't be able to understand anything else he had to say. This one was the measuring stick because the "seed" represented the Word of God. See, predating even the Rosetta stone, God has a standard, and it is found in the Bible. Everything else is measured by it.

ENGAGING HEAVEN

Isn't it interesting that all the grass, trees, and most of the food we eat comes from a seed? Seeds, like the Word of God, are truly life-giving.

Rooted in Love

Though I have the gift of prophecy,
and understand all mysteries and all knowledge,
and though I have all faith, so that I could remove mountains,
but have not love, I am nothing.

1 CORINTHIANS 13:2 NKJV

We are only as strong as our roots, and the Bible says to
be rooted in love (Ephesians 3:17). A firm foundation is
everything. Only a fool builds her house on the sand because
sand is unpredictable and shifting. A wise woman builds
her house on rock (Matthew 7:24–27), and the greatest,
strongest, most reliable rock is Jesus Christ. Philippians 1:21
reassures us that to die is our gain. Why? Because we gain
Christ. If we spend our life chasing money, to die is a loss
because we don't take our money with us. If we spend our
life building a business, to die is a loss because that business
will fall into new hands. Even if we spend our whole lives
serving our family and we put our identity into that, to die is
loss because we go on without our family. Our hope is not in
our money or our business or our family. Our hope is in Christ
alone. Stay rooted in Christ and his love.

ENGAGING HEAVEN

*How does choosing Christ before your family equip you
to better love and serve your family?*

There Is Always a Cost

"If anyone desires to come after Me,
let him deny himself,
and take up his cross, and follow Me."
MATTHEW 16:24 NKJV

Jesus paid for everything at Calvary, but that doesn't mean it costs us nothing to follow him. Everything has a price associated with it, yet a lot of people live as if they don't have a part to play. There is a cost to obedience and a cost to disobedience, and the cost of disobedience will be far greater. Unforgiveness, for example, has a huge price tag, and it could include hell. Hatred, jealousy, rage, and offense will cost us our peace, relationships, and even our sleep and health. They are simply not worth the cost. It's a high price for a low level of living. We've all been hurt, but don't allow yourself to stoop into an expensive pit of loathing. When trauma comes, determine that your peace is not for sale. Give it to Jesus.

ENGAGING HEAVEN

If you've gone as far as you can go in your current level of surrender, then it is time to go to the inner room. The entrance fee is love.

Single for a Reason

If you want to reign in life, don't sit on your hands.
Instead, work hard at doing what's right,
for the slacker will end up working
to make someone else succeed.

PROVERBS 12:24 TPT

There is not a woman alive who is sitting at home, praying, *Lord, please send me a man who doesn't shower. I want a guy who smells and who's lazy too.* She doesn't exist. So, why would God want smelly, lazy people either? He uses people who show effort and are ready to rule. If we want to rule and experience breakthrough, if we want increase, then we must be diligent. We have to do little things every day to get to where we want to be. Faith looks at the mountain and, instead of becoming discouraged, starts planning a way to conquer it. People who thrive for God don't do so by accident or luck. We can't claim to have a relationship with God if we're not willing to devote even just fifteen uninterrupted minutes with him daily. Make daily decisions and be diligent. In time, God will transform your life. Diligent hands rule in the end.

ENGAGING HEAVEN

What commitments have you made to the Lord? What commitments have you made to your family or to your church? it's important that we be trustworthy and do what we say we'll do.

When the Sun Sets

"Be angry, and do not sin":
do not let the sun go down on your wrath.
EPHESIANS 4:26 NKJV

Don't go to bed angry. Don't let yesterday's problems leak into today. It's a new day. It's a new morning. Every time the sun rises, it's new grace and mercy. We have to take this life with the Lord one day at a time. Forgive yesterday's offenses, move past the hurt, and praise God for today. Let's not let one moment of today's joy be robbed because of pain from the past or anxiety about the future. When times get tough, we continue to love. We continue to trust the Lord and focus on him. We're not going to get today again; there are no re-dos. The storms of life will most certainly come, and while we may bend, we will not break if our eyes are fixed on Jesus and if we are not bearing the additional loads of yesterday and tomorrow. We can't look back or hold on to regret if we're going to maximize today's blessings.

ENGAGING HEAVEN

Today, tell somebody how much they mean to you.

The Storm between Your Ears

"Far be it from You to...
slay the righteous with the wicked...
Shall not the Judge of all the earth do right?"
GENESIS 18:25 NKJV

There are so many "spiritual meteorologists" these days claiming that the many natural disasters we've endured is evidence that God is sending his judgment on America. Honestly, the real storm is between their ears. Do you really believe if God were judging America, he would send a hurricane? That's his ace in the hole? That is a weak form of judgment. Those who have read the Bible know that when God sends judgment on a place, it is completely leveled and left barren. Yes, God was angry, but what was his remedy? Jesus. He sent his Son to take our judgment. *That* is the nature of our Father in heaven. Not understanding God's nature hinders us from moving forward because we think every rainstorm is a sign that he's judging us. Do you know why your city won't experience full judgment? Because you're there. God would have been willing to spare Sodom and Gomorrah for the sake of ten people who loved him, and he's still on the lookout for those who will stand in the gap.

ENGAGING HEAVEN

If we don't understand God's loving nature, it leaves us open and exposed to life's storms. There is a canopy of protection and power for God's people.

Unholy Matrimony

Draw near to God and He will draw near to you.
Cleanse your hands, you sinners;
and purify your hearts, you double-minded.
JAMES 4:8 NKJV

People are not staying committed to each other because they're not staying committed to God. How can we honor a relationship in the natural when we're not honoring God's relationship first? If you have a husband, make sure your relationship with God is the strongest there is *so that* your relationship with your husband can be strong as well. If you are a mother, daughter, sister, coworker, best friend, or have any other relational role, keep in mind that your relationships are only going to be as strong as your relationship with God is. If you're not staying connected to the source of love himself, God, how can you pour love into all the other important relationships in your life? We live in a disconnected world, and marriages are suffering at the altar of disobedience and disconnect. The breakdowns we see in society are a spiritual issue. They're caused by a deficit of sacrificial love and a spiritual wound. We need to start honoring our relationships again, starting with our relationship with Jesus.

ENGAGING HEAVEN

How do you show God your commitment to your relationship with him?

Daughter of the King

May we never forget that Yahweh works wonders
for every one of his devoted lovers.
And this is how I know that he will answer my every prayer.
PSALM 4:3 TPT

Because you're a daughter of the living God, you were not created to slave at a job. You were not placed on earth to simply be born in a crib and die in a box. He specifically and perfectly crafted you to touch this world for Christ. Your ministry may be formal or informal and will vary based on what you do, where you are, and who you're around. But you were still intended for far more than just a job. God knew you in your mother's womb, and he formed you uniquely with giftings and passions that only he knows completely. When you engage in those gifts, you begin to step into the fullness of what God has called you to. Always remember that you are a daughter of the Most High King, and he always hears and always answers your prayers.

ENGAGING HEAVEN

What do you think you specifically were created to do?
What are some of your gifts and passions?

Rosebush Lessons

In Him you also trusted, after you heard the word of truth,
the gospel of your salvation;
in whom also, having believed,
you were sealed with the Holy Spirit of promise.
EPHESIANS 1:13 NKJV

A rosebush can represent people who have been through difficult times but who will grow buds again because rosebushes are resilient. Even the winter frost can't kill them, and they will blossom again in the spring. And even though you've been through hard seasons, the devil is not able to kill you either because the love of Christ flows through your veins. You're going to get back up, and you're going to bloom again. The Bible says that "He who has begun a good work in you will complete it until the day of Jesus Christ" (Philippians 1:6 NKJV). It is God who initiated this work in you, and he's not going to give up because of a little winter frost. He will complete what he started. Jesus is "the Alpha and the Omega, the Beginning and the End" (Revelation 21:6 NKJV), the First and the Last. He started all of creation, and he will finish it. Life might be hard right now; maybe all you see is a bunch of thorns, but keep the faith because spring is coming again.

ENGAGING HEAVEN

Flourishing doesn't happen overnight, so be patient.
In time, with love and care and watering,
your thorns will turn to roses again.

Opportunity

"If you can believe,
all things are possible to him who believes."
MARK 9:23 NKJV

When was the last time you had ventured out and believed the impossible? When was the last time you walked on water? When was the last time it was just you and God alone, without distractions? People of faith live in that realm. Comfort has become a cancer to Christianity. For many Christians, it has been a long time since they stretched their faith, prayed boldly for somebody, or took a step off the edge into the arms of God. There's fruit available for everyone that many people will never know exists because it's only reached through embracing opportunity. It's not a lack of open doors; rather it's a lack of seeing and seizing the opportunities before you. People who serve the kingdom see things that people who serve themselves could never imagine. It only comes with honoring God and giving all to Jesus.

ENGAGING HEAVEN

What opportunities has God given you?

Power with a Purpose

"Indeed for this purpose I have raised you up,
that I may show My power in you,
and that My name may be declared in all the earth."

Exodus 9:16 NKJV

If every day of your life is the same routine and nothing changes, be careful because you might find yourself without spiritual legs to walk toward what God is calling you to do. We say we're living for eternity, but somehow, we've fallen victim to this self-pleasing, self-seeking culture. Yes, God loves you, but it's not about you. This life is a fleeting moment. It's not even the most significant thing that we live for. So many people live dead routines with no dream and no vision. But God wants to raise us up and demonstrate his power through us! We need to raise our expectations for life to another level. God is looking for people with a God-sized dream that he can fulfill. We need a purpose to experience his power, so dream, believe, and raise your expectations.

ENGAGING HEAVEN

*If God said he wanted to put his power in you,
what would you do with it?*

The Price of Sacrifice

"No, but I will surely buy it from you for a price;
nor will I offer burnt offerings to the LORD my God
with that which costs me nothing."

2 SAMUEL 24:24 NKJV

We want things fast and convenient. We are so motivated by results and don't have a lot of patience for them. Culturally, we have grown to not like resistance and will do what we can to avoid it. But the truth is, if we want to experience real breakthrough, it's going to require work. This is evident in the area of health and fitness, but it is even more true in our spiritual health and growth. King David purchased a threshing floor and oxen so he could sacrifice to God. Araunah was willing to gift everything to the king for free, but David refused, saying he wasn't going to offer the Lord something that didn't cost him anything. See, true sacrifice has a price associated with it. When it comes to the things of God, there's no cheap way through. It's going to cost us everything. The things we're believing for today are going to cost us, so let's hold fast, stand our ground, and be ready to surrender everything to God.

ENGAGING HEAVEN

What have you sacrificed to follow God?

What's in Your Heart?

"He who does not take his cross and follow
after Me is not worthy of Me.
He who finds his life will lose it,
and he who loses his life for My sake will find it."
Matthew 10:38–39 NKJV

If you ask any child what they want to be when they grow up, they may say they want to be a firefighter or a police officer or a princess. None of them would claim they want to work hard and then die. Children dream and have lofty goals. And why not? At what point do we stop dreaming and live discouraged? Why were you created? What purpose does God have for you? If you knew you couldn't fail and resources were endless, what would you aspire to do? Would you lay hands on the sick in a hospital? Would you feed the poor? Perhaps you would go on mission trips. The truth is, so many people are not filling their time with what is in their heart to do. And that's a big trap. Your job can be a trap if it steals you away from God's calling on your life.

ENGAGING HEAVEN

It's time to set some goals. It is time to stand on your feet again. It's time to believe God, live boldly, and line your dreams up with what you're doing today.

Tongue Trap

Your words are so powerful
that they will kill or give life,
and the talkative person will reap
the consequences.
PROVERBS 18:21 TPT

The power of life and death are in your tongue, and whether you realize it or not, you create your world with your words. Your life—either wonderful or terrible—may have a lot to do with your words. God created this world with his words, and we create ours today similarly. The Bible says your tongue is like a rudder steering a ship (James 3:4). Being a Christian and having faith means you can speak confidently from a world that isn't here. When you pray for somebody, you're praying for something that has not manifested yet, but you believe it will. But if you're only complaining, it will drain your life, your energy, and your friends. Complaining is a cancer. Instead of looking for the worst-case scenario, hope for the best. Don't respond to your spouse or your best friend negatively because you want them to meet a need that only God can fill. Take responsibility and realize that your tongue holds a lot of power.

ENGAGING HEAVEN

*I challenge you to go one day with no complaints.
Speak only life and see God move in the midst.*

Overcoming Offense

Love overlooks the mistakes of others,
but dwelling on the failures of others
devastates friendships.
PROVERBS 17:9 TPT

When somebody hurts you or misunderstands you, don't
give the enemy a place in your heart. Go back to that person
and work things out so the enemy never gets a foothold in
it. Even if the other person is unwilling to work with you to
make things right, you have done your part, and the devil can
no longer haunt you with it. Ultimately, our identity needs
to be established in Christ because, when it is, it will be far
harder for anyone to offend you. As long as your feeling of
security is rooted in yourself, the tendency to take offense
is always going to be there. First Peter 4:8 says, "Love will
cover a multitude of sins" (NKJV). It doesn't say that love
will help you muster up the courage to forgive once...it says
"a multitude"! Many, many little sins and hurts and offenses.
That's how strong love is. Your heart is not worth being lost
to offense. The invitation to be offended is always going to
be there, so choose love. Choose freedom. Choose God.

ENGAGING HEAVEN

Where is your security found?

The Best You

Whatever your hand finds to do, do it with your might;
for there is no work or device or knowledge or wisdom
in the grave where you are going.

ECCLESIASTES 9:10 NKJV

Nothing gets accomplished well when we're trying to do too many things. When we're too busy, we become distracted from the things that matter. We live perpetually distracted from what God is really calling us to do because we don't have time to listen. The tricky part is we're distracted with good things. It's easy to justify and believe we're doing the work of God, but "good" is the enemy of "great," and even "great" is the enemy of "best." God wants the best version of you. Your family, your church, your work...everyone else would benefit from the best version of you too. They won't get that if you're constantly rundown, exhausted, cranky, frustrated, and distracted. It might be time to cut some good things out of your life so you can be stronger, more focused, and work with all your might toward the best things in your life. Are you living the best life that God has for you?

ENGAGING HEAVEN

*What if the devil wanted to pull you away from church?
How would he do it? Could he perhaps give you an increase
at your job or a new opportunity? Could something good
distract you from God's best?*

When God Answers

> "Ask, and it will be given to you;
> seek, and you will find;
> knock, and it will be opened to you."
>
> MATTHEW 7:7 NKJV

In Acts 12, the early believers were all at Mary's house praying for Peter to get out of prison. Peter got out, came to the door, knocked, and they saw him, shut the door in his face, and continued to pray for him. They forgot to invite God to the prayer meeting, apparently. When we pray, are we simply offering up sweet sentiments out of Christian duty, or do we believe God actually hears and is prepared to answer? Some people see money as a sign of the blessing of the Lord. Sure, money *could* be, but it isn't necessarily. There are many wealthy people who obtained their fortunes through corrupt means. Other people believe that feeling good and comfortable is a sign that God is blessing them. Again, this isn't necessarily a sign of God's favor. What happens when their comfort is disrupted? Has God suddenly become unfavorable? No, God is more than a feeling. Nothing replaces the Word of God, hearing his voice, seeing his miracles, and praying. Listen for that knock on your door.

ENGAGING HEAVEN

*Why do you think those early believers were unprepared
to see God actually answer their prayers for Peter?
What are you praying for? Are you seeking signs,
or are you seeking God?*

True Treasure

"Lay up for yourselves treasures in heaven,
where neither moth nor rust destroys
and where thieves do not break in and steal.
For where your treasure is,
there your heart will be also."

Matthew 6:20–21 NKJV

An idol is anything that steals our attention and devotion from Christ's image. We might not be worshiping a golden calf anymore, but we absolutely settle for idols on this earth. We can even fall more in love with ministry than with our Maker. It's important that we refuse to allow anything material to distract us from the true treasure of knowing Jesus Christ. We can't simply say that he's Lord of our lives and then worship other things. Jesus warned us that "when you pray, you shall not be like the hypocrites. For they love to pray standing in the synagogues and on the corners of the streets, that they may be seen by men. Assuredly, I say to you, they have their reward" (v. 5 NKJV). Our true treasure and real rewards are waiting for us in heaven. If we work to impress others instead of serve God, we've received our reward already.

ENGAGING HEAVEN

What reward are you seeking?

Wrong Choices

When Yahweh delights in how you live your life,
he establishes your every step.

PSALM 37:23 TPT

A lot of people have a hard time making decisions because they are scared to make wrong choices. They don't know how to make their "yes be yes" and their "no be no" (Matthew 5:37). Our God is a loving Father who doesn't condemn us for our mistakes. He takes our hands and helps us navigate them. If we listen to the Lord and walk in his ways, he will guide us and bless us. Because of this promise to us, we don't have to be double-minded or live in a place of indecision. God equips us with the confidence to make bold choices and take risks. If we walked around in life always scared that we are going to make the wrong choices, how can we ever move forward and accomplish anything worthwhile? It's so much better to take God's hand and walk boldly down the path. If we go the wrong way, he will lead us back. If we stumble, he will catch us. But either way, we're moving forward into a life of no regrets.

ENGAGING HEAVEN

Are you scared to take a step toward something?
Ask God to take your hand. He delights in you!

Unchanging Truth

For through the eternal and living Word of God
you have been born again.
And this "seed" that he planted within you
can never be destroyed
but will live and grow inside you forever.
1 PETER 1:23 TPT

Truth is truth. Right is right, wrong is wrong, and it's never right to do wrong. Truth reveals Jesus, which empowers us to live victoriously. When we don't listen to or obey the truth, we end up living defeated lives. Despite the blood that was shed and the incredible price Christ paid, we still hang our heads in defeat, looking at our circumstances instead of at the cross. But the cross was more than enough. Instead of acting defeated, we should be lifting our head because we are victorious in Christ. The gold medal is ours... it's time we act like it. Let's lift our heads and praise God through whatever circumstances we're facing today, because whatever they are, the cross is still more than enough. The battle has already been won, and we win. When we know the outcome, it gives us faith to stand and continue pressing on.

ENGAGING HEAVEN

Do you still act defeated, or have you accepted your gold medal? Do your circumstances determine your condition or does the cross?

Glorious Treasure Within

We are like common clay jars
that carry this glorious treasure within,
so that this immeasurable power
will be seen as God's, not ours.
2 CORINTHIANS 4:7 TPT

When the devil tries to destroy you and tear you down and make you feel worthless, when you feel like there's no hope, remember there is a glorious treasure within you. Remember the deposit of Jesus is in you, the value of which is tremendous. Too many believers act like they're condemned, but they're really the carriers of Christ's immeasurable power. Open your eyes and recognize the value of who you are by leaning into Jesus. When you see how big God is and you receive the love of the Father, the worth you perceive in yourself goes up. You start to value yourself when you understand how greatly God values you. You're either going to let God set your worth or the world. It will never be both. The enemy is always trying to remind you of who you used to be whereas the Father is telling you who you are.

ENGAGING HEAVEN

The value of something is determined by what someone is willing to pay for it, and Jesus paid his life for you.

Protecting Sweet

It is easier to conquer a strong city
than to win back a friend whom you've offended.
Their walls go up, making it nearly impossible
to win them back.
PROVERBS 18:19 TPT

We were all born with trust and hope. We started off in life sweet and beautiful, vulnerable and innocent. This world is cruel, however, and time tarnishes. We get hurt and offended, and it's very hard to come back from offense. We can't lose that sweetness, though, because otherwise we end up cranky, frustrated, and unlikeable. Offense blocks us from seeing clearly and makes everything appear like it's in contention. The Lord put that original sweetness in us, and it's worth defending. It's worth fighting for. If we lose it, it's hard to get it back, but God is willing to restore it. Offense is a prison, and sweetness is our freedom. When our hearts stay tender and open, we can walk in hope and love, trusting God and seeing the best in others. Protect that. If you've lost it, ask God to help you get it back. It's worth it.

ENGAGING HEAVEN

*Do you have sweetness in your heart? If so, protect it.
If not, ask God to help you restore it.*

False Finish Lines

He was transfigured before them.
His face shone like the sun,
and His clothes became as white as the light.
MATTHEW 17:2 NKJV

Mistakes you made in your past may hold you back, but what surprisingly holds a lot of people back is their past successes. When Jesus was transfigured and Moses and Elijah appeared, Peter offered to build three tabernacles for them. He was so enamored by what was going on, but it was over just as quickly. What Peter didn't realize was that, as incredible as this encounter was, the best was still to come. If he had stayed on that mountain reveling in that experience, he would have missed all the incredible things God still had in store for him. It would have been a false finish because Jesus was just getting warmed up. So many people want the "good old days" and to relive the moments that moved them. They want the honeymoon stage back in their marriages, failing to see how their union has grown over time. There's a reason the sun goes down and rises again every morning.

ENGAGING HEAVEN

*Are you dwelling too much on your past successes,
or are you ready to go forward into even greater days?*

Original Recipe

As for God, His way is perfect;
The word of the LORD is proven;
He is a shield to all who trust in Him.
PSALM 18:30 NKJV

There is a recipe that God has ordained for us to follow, and it would be foolish to try to alter it. We need to stand solid on what has always worked and not replace it with the watered-down version the enemy is producing. The devil wants you to think that truth has changed, that it's influenced by culture, but that is not the case. The Word of God has stood the tests of time and proven to be reliable and flawless. We shouldn't be adding to or removing from the original recipe because it cannot be improved upon. Truth never changes. People are trying to redefine what truth is and even attempt to make it subjective by calling it "your truth" and "my truth." They'll say things like, "What's true for you might not be true for me," but that's not truth...those are merely opinions. Truth stands alone. Despite what is popular, accepted, or sounds good, truth is unchanging and unyielding. We can't change what has always been to fit our preference.

ENGAGING HEAVEN

Are you going to live by God's original recipe or by the world's trends?

Rat Race

Martha was distracted with much serving,
and she approached Him and said,
"Lord, do You not care that my sister
has left me to serve alone?
Therefore tell her to help me."

Luke 10:40 NKJV

Somewhere along the line, being busy became a status symbol. Filling our time up makes us feel more important to ourselves and others. We have slowly, as a society, become more preoccupied than ever before. But busyness isn't a virtue. Rather, it's a sign of instability and doesn't leave us open to God's improvisations. If our values are right, we'll find time is worth more than money. The trouble with being in the rat race is that even when we win, we're still rats. The goal isn't to fill our time; it's to be effective, right? If we're slaves to the clock or the to-do list, how are we going to be fruitful or enjoy all the wonderful gifts God has given us? Be productive, be fruitful, be present with the ones you love. Stop robbing yourself of the greatest things in life.

ENGAGING HEAVEN

Do you have time for your family? Do you play with your children? Do you talk with your spouse undistracted? Do you talk with your friends and have meaningful relationships? Are you just running through life in a blur?

Unending Hope

Now may the God of hope fill you
with all joy and peace in believing,
that you may abound in hope
by the power of the Holy Spirit.
ROMANS 15:13 NKJV

There's a creative realm of heaven filled with supply: all the things we're lacking right now. It is available for us if we just confess it. Why don't we start there instead of declaring death and hurt? Why not assume God is a generous, loving Father instead of a stingy, easily angered one? After all, God can do anything he wants, and he loves us. So, we don't need to live in a dark place with no hope. This earth has no hope outside of Jesus. Life is bleak without Jesus but full of hope and light with him. And because we're the ones who know him, it should be *us* influencing the atmosphere and changing the world instead of the world influencing and changing us. It's time for us to shine the light of Jesus and spread hope, clinging to truth, and casting off all darkness and lies.

ENGAGING HEAVEN

When you have a conversation with someone, do your words spread dismay or hope?

March

Seek God, Not Goodies

"You shall have no other gods before Me."
EXODUS 20:3 NKJV

We have many things that occupy our time, money, thoughts, and attention. If we're not careful and intentional, these things will take over our lives and push God out. We must learn to prioritize God before everything. After all, he's the reason for everything we do. The earth isn't orbiting around us. We are all orbiting around the Lord. True, your boss, teacher, husband, kids, and friends are all clamoring for your attention, but you're only as strong for everyone else as you are with the Lord. The world will empty you, and only God can truly fill you. It's all about priorities. Maybe you have deadlines or hungry kids, but if you make God the priority in your life, everything else will fall into place—truly. Yes, we all have responsibilities, but don't allow life to bog you down. Start with God so you can take on the rest of life fulfilled, rejuvenated, strong, and focused. Seek him first always.

ENGAGING HEAVEN

What in your life comes before God? How can you shift this around so your priorities are where they're supposed to be?

Fully Preaching

In mighty signs and wonders,
by the power of the Spirit of God...
I have fully preached the gospel of Christ.
ROMANS 15:19 NKJV

If Paul wrote, "By baking cookies and giving them out on Wednesday nights, we fully preached the gospel," churches all over the world would be baking cookies. If Paul claimed, "By knitting sweaters for nursing homes, we fully preach the gospel," everybody would pick up knitting. But he said, "In mighty signs and wonders, by the power of the Spirit of God." That means we can't do it on our own. That means we need God's power at work in our lives because cookies and sweaters alone are not going to get the job done. Spreading the gospel requires surrender, devouring the Word, being hungry for him. It requires us to get over ourselves and get back to what matters. This gospel has not changed. It still has the power to set free the captives, the depressed, the addicted, and the broken. It still has the power to deliver and heal. *We* are the ones who have changed. It's time to get back to loving God, honoring God, and going after him with reckless abandonment.

ENGAGING HEAVEN

The question is, are you fully preaching?

Power of Distraction

This I say for your own profit,
not that I may put a leash on you,
but for what is proper, and that you may
serve the Lord without distraction.

1 CORINTHIANS 7:35 NKJV

The power of distraction is a weapon of mass destruction. It will destroy your productivity and your potential. We get so distracted, especially when we have so many options at our fingertips. People do better when afforded fewer options, which is why Christianity has always flourished in the face of persecution. With more access and more opportunities to take the easy path, it becomes significantly harder to stay disciplined. Distraction is the enemy of discipleship. In this age of social media and connection in the world, people are suffering from loneliness. Use the internet for greatness, but make sure it's serving you instead of you serving it. The Bible also says, "For every idle word men may speak, they will give account of it in the day of judgment" (Matthew 12:36 NKJV), and that includes what you post. Be careful; do not lose your integrity. Limit your distractions.

ENGAGING HEAVEN

How much time do you spend each day on your phone or computer? How much time do you spend in prayer?

You Are a Debtor

I am a debtor both to Greeks and to barbarians,
both to wise and to unwise.

ROMANS 1:14 NKJV

What did Paul mean in saying that he was a debtor? What he was declaring was that, because of the love and forgiveness God had shown him, he now had an obligation to share that love and forgiveness with everyone else. God cleared such an enormous, impossible debt from each of us, and the only recompense he requires is that we share his love with others. You are a debtor to your family, your children, and everyone else—not because they deserve it but because God does. If you have children, you owe it to God to make sure that your children encounter him through you. You owe it to God to be an example of his love at your business, your school, your church, even driving in traffic. Wherever you go, whatever you do, remember what you have been called to. This world is hurting, and the answer is not another political party. It's Christ in you. We must allow God to have his way in our lives.

ENGAGING HEAVEN

Who can you show God's love to today and, in doing so, show God your love for him?

Stand on the Word

Do not be unwise,
but understand what the will of the Lord is.
EPHESIANS 5:17 NKJV

Renewed minds prove the will of God. When your mind is renewed, you can step into God's will, which is unquestionably the best for your life. We know what the will of God is by what the Word of God says. Simply put, the will of the Lord is the Word of the Lord in your life. It's fine if you've never heard a prophetic word from God. Just read the Bible and grab hold of every promise that it says. Stand on these promises daily. Then if God gives you a prophetic word, that's great! It supplements what is already in your heart. You don't need to look for an external word to confirm the Word of God. Scripture is already enough to stand on. And pray Scripture. When you pray, you'll begin to think differently, and your mind will be renewed because God will put his desires in you.

ENGAGING HEAVEN

Prayer is a moment where your mind is off the world and you are listening to a different voice. Let God speak to you through prayer and through his Word.

Give Me the Mountain

"I am as strong this day as on the day that Moses sent me;
...Now therefore, give me this mountain...
It may be that the LORD will be with me."
JOSHUA 14:11–12 NKJV

The Israelites were dividing up the land, and Caleb said he'd take the mountain. It seemed like a questionable endeavor since the land was difficult and fortified with the Anakim, and Caleb was eighty-five years old. What are most eighty-five-year-olds doing? Sitting at home, watching television, remembering the "good old days." Caleb, on the other hand, said, "Give me the mountain." He was still conquering lands. At eighty-five, he still served the same God he did when he was forty, and he was confident that, since his victory came from the Lord who doesn't change, he would have victory again. Who says you've already lived your best life or that your greatest days are behind you? They are behind you only if you *think* they are. If you had nothing left to live for or your purpose was over, God would have already brought you home. Purpose doesn't age out. It's either accomplished or it isn't. There's more work to do and your greatest days may still be ahead of you.

ENGAGING HEAVEN

Do you believe in your heart that your greatest days are still to come? How is that reflected in the way you live?

Reset Button

"Through the tender mercy of our God,
With which the Dayspring from on high has visited us;
To give light to those who sit in darkness
and the shadow of death,
To guide our feet into the way of peace."

Luke 1:78-79 NKJV

Sometimes God wants us to start anew and hit the reset button on faith. Maybe you have had a long time of walking with Jesus and studying the Bible. Perhaps you even teach and counsel others. But it's possible for your wisdom and your teachings over the years to have taught you out of the realm of faith. Do you recall those new sparks of being a young Christian when you'd discover a new truth about Jesus? Time and knowledge can deaden your faith and hinder you from hearing the new things God is trying to tell you. Maybe everything you think is making you wise is actually clogging you up and inviting pride into your heart. Remember that God cares about you and about all the little things you are facing. Hit the reset button today and listen. He has a fresh message for you today.

ENGAGING HEAVEN

*What has God been teaching you recently
about his tender mercy?*

Where Are You?

The Lord God called to Adam and said to him,
"Where are you?"
Genesis 3:9 NKJV

When God asked Adam where he was, God already knew the answer. But did Adam? This is an important question for us to ask ourselves regularly. At every junction in our lives, if we're committed to staying in the will of God, we need to check ourselves and ask, *Where am I? Where am I spiritually located? Am I where I'm supposed to be? Have I moved from the last place God told me to be?* If we're not where we're supposed to be, it's time to get back to that place. Leave! Run! To whatever is needed to realign with God's will. This is how we find peace, make a difference, draw closer to God, and find our purpose. Ask yourself this question from time to time to evaluate if you've drifted to the left or the right or become sidetracked by anything less than God's perfect design for your life. He will direct you if you're willing to follow.

ENGAGING HEAVEN

Where are you?

Healthy Decisions

The women also who serve the church
should be dignified, faithful in all things,
having their thoughts set on truth,
and not known as those who gossip.

1 Timothy 3:11 TPT

A deflated marriage is rarely a blown tire. It's almost always
a slow leak. There is no such thing as one great, defining
decision in life. Those are always preceded by a series
of smaller, good choices. We have to spend a long time
stretching and practicing before we can make a leap great
enough to get us to the place we want to be. There is also
no such thing as one big, bad decision that ruins everything;
there really isn't. If the fall was that hard, it was surely
preceded by a procession of smaller, poor decisions that
ultimately brought about the final fall. This principle is true
in life, but it is especially true in marriage. Rarely is one giant
gesture enough to keep a heart or one monstrous mistake
enough to lose a heart. All those little moments and decisions
lead to being the spouse we are today.

ENGAGING HEAVEN

*Sometimes we see others' success or their amazing
marriages and think they just got lucky, but they actually put
a lot of hard, unrecognized work into setting themselves up
for it. What small steps are you taking today that will impact
your future?*

Still the Pearl

She is more precious than rubies,
and all the things you may desire
cannot compare with her.
PROVERBS 3:15 NKJV

Everything has a cost associated with it. Sin has a *huge* price tag. Countless marriages dissolve because somebody made a sinful gamble. It could have been just for a few minutes, but it destroyed things forever. The cost of sin will always be death. Breakthrough and healing have a price. Yes, everything was paid for on the cross, but that doesn't mean we don't have a part to play now. Matthew 13:46 tells the story of a merchant "who, when he had found one pearl of great price, went and sold all that he had and bought it" (NKJV). He recognized the value of this pearl was superior to everything else he owned. Well, there's still a kingdom today worth giving everything for. There is still a King worth giving everything for.

ENGAGING HEAVEN

What cost are you willing to pay for Jesus?

Women of Faith

Charm is deceitful and beauty is passing,
but a woman who fears the LORD,
she shall be praised.

PROVERBS 31:30 NKJV

Sarah considered, Hannah contended, and Mary surrendered. These powerful women of faith lived in such a way that it can still encourage us today. Constantly consistent, Sarah considered God faithful to his promises even though what he was promising seemed outrageous. Her faith gave her strength to do the impossible: conceive and birth a child in her old age (Hebrews 11:11). Hannah contended for the promises of God, did not complain, did not turn to the left or the right, and instead sought her Maker. She poured her soul out before God, and he rewarded her with a child despite her barrenness (1 Samuel 1:20). In the face of the weightiest assignment ever given to a young girl, regardless of the guaranteed judgment and risk, and despite the known and unknown challenges ahead of her, Mary surrendered herself to the Lord's will (Luke 1:28). In doing so, she became the mother of the Lord and Savior of all mankind...Jesus Christ.

ENGAGING HEAVEN

What encouragement do you draw from these women's testimonies?

Power Source

"Is not My word like a fire?" says the LORD,
"And like a hammer that breaks the rock in pieces?"
JEREMIAH 23:29 NKJV

Many Christians are attracted to the idea of the Holy Spirit but not the manifestation of him in their lives. What we're plugged in to shows, however, and what we're doing privately will reveal itself in time. If we want to be great for God, we need to plug in to the power of the Holy Spirit. That is what the attraction is to a lost and dying world. The anointing of God matters. Being authentic matters, and all the other extracurricular stuff is nothing more than clanging cymbals. To make an impact on this earth and leave a mark for God, we need to stay plugged in. Going through life's battles will certainly prove what we're plugged in to. Are you plugged in to the Lord and his Word? Are you spending time with him? Are you fellowshiping? Yes, the cross finished everything for us, but we still need to receive what Jesus paid for and walk in a love relationship with him.

ENGAGING HEAVEN

A lack of power is directly connected to a lack of relationship.

Trending Topics

"For whoever desires to save his life will lose it,
but whoever loses his life for My sake will find it."
MATTHEW 16:25 NKJV

Christianity is not a gospel that allows us to pick and choose what we want. It's not a salad where we can add what we like and remove whatever we don't like. He's not a "good Father" in the sense that he's going to just ignore and forget our sin. He's a "good Father" who addresses our sin so as to keep us within the confines of protection so we don't fall into bondage or defile our souls. That's the good Father we serve. We don't wake up in the morning and wonder what we believe or wonder if God is with us. The gospel is clear and straightforward, and there's no reason we need to add or subtract from it. If you really want to walk with Jesus, repent, surrender, embrace heaven, pray every day, talk to God, read your Bible, and live right. You can't live wrong and die right.

ENGAGING HEAVEN

Do you approach the Bible like a buffet, choosing what you
want and what you don't, or do you approach it like the law
of God you live your life by?

Don't Quit

If your faith remains strong,
even while surrounded by life's difficulties,
you will continue to experience the untold blessings of God!
True happiness comes as you pass the test with faith,
and receive the victorious crown of life
promised to every lover of God!
JAMES 1:12 TPT

Breakthrough is found in resistance. Instead of looking at the challenges and problems of life as attacks from the devil, consider that perhaps God has more in store for you than the comfortable normal you've grown accustomed to. Maybe the aches and pains are really God's way of saying, "You're close! Push through! Don't quit because I have so much more for you." Remember the reason you fell in love with Jesus to begin with and find that flame again. Breakthrough is right around the corner from resistance. Create habits in your life, and little by little, you *will* make it through the resistance you're facing, but only if you don't quit. An elephant is eaten one bite at a time, right? Stop trying to go somewhere you're not ready for yet. Believe God today, put one foot in front of the other, and realize that what you're doing will lead you where you want to go in time.

ENGAGING HEAVEN

What new habits do you plan to implement
in your life this week?

Pruning

"Every branch in Me that does not bear fruit He takes away;
and every branch that bears fruit He prunes,
that it may bear more fruit."
JOHN 15:2 NKJV

We don't like pruning. We don't like trials. We don't enjoy
the storms of life, although there's no getting around them.
Storms happen to the best people in the world because
we all live in this world. They're inevitable. Matthew 5:45
says, "He...sends rain on the just and on the unjust" (NKJV).
It doesn't matter how benevolent or evil we are; if we're
outside during a rainstorm, we're going to get wet. We live
in this fallen world, and most of our lives are affected by
other people's decisions. Plain and simple: life is not fair. If
you're married, you know this is true. If you're a mother, you
definitely know it's true. We look at trials as a bad thing,
almost like a sign that something is not right, but that is just
simply not the case. When we are faithful and bear fruit, God
will prune us so we can be even *more* faithful and bring forth
more fruit.

ENGAGING HEAVEN

*How often do you do little things for your husband (or your
mom or your roommate) or fix someone's mistakes without
anyone recognizing it? How grateful are your children or
your coworkers for all the work you do for them? God sees.*

Unsocial Media

All things are lawful for me,
but not all things are helpful;
all things are lawful for me,
but not all things edify.
1 CORINTHIANS 10:23 NKJV

Social media has made us more unsocial. There's no doubt about it. There are many areas in which social media is helpful, but we need to temper and control our use of it. As soon as social media starts to control you instead of you controlling it, it has become too much. Sure, having social media accounts may be permitted, but that doesn't mean it's good for us. The evidence that social media has made us a lot less social is clear to see. We invest less time in real friendships, have fewer meaningful face-to-face conversations, and are becoming more reclusive in nature. It's easy to hide behind a screen and not let people into our real lives. We don't show our faces as often. In fact, we walk around staring down at our phones, not even looking up anymore. A lot of the beauty of real, authentic, naturally occurring relationships is being lost and replaced by a barrage of picture-perfect profiles—carefully crafted to create whatever illusion the owner desires to depict. Social media in itself is not wrong, but we can use it wrong.

ENGAGING HEAVEN

Do you limit your time on social media and invest in real, face-to-face relationships?

Open Your Eyes

I pray that the Father of Glory,
the God of our Lord Jesus Christ,
would impart to you the riches of the
Spirit of wisdom and the Spirit of revelation
to know him through your deepening intimacy with him.
EPHESIANS 1:17 TPT

Who has God placed around you? Who are your friends?
Who has he given you as mentors? Embrace those
relationships. When you start longing for and being jealous
of somebody else's mentor, somebody else's friends,
somebody else's husband, it leads to discontent and spiritual
death. What has God given you? What talents, resources,
and accesses has God trusted you with? The same rule
applies. Instead of wishing you had what someone else has,
open your eyes and recognize how incredibly blessed you
are. Focus your attention on the gifts you *have* been given
and get the most out of them. Focus your energy on the
relationships active in your life right now and see them for
the blessing that they are. That's when you'll really start to
experience the abundant life God has surrounded you with.

ENGAGING HEAVEN

*Hold your loved ones close today and use the gifts God
has given specifically to you.*

Be Holy

"Be holy, for I am holy."
1 PETER 1:16 NKJV

James 1:14 says that "each one is tempted when he is drawn away by his own desires and enticed" (NKJV). Desire is the beginning of sin because every bad behavior starts with a desire. Desires aren't always bad, and temptation is inevitable, but sin happens when we accept the invitation and give in to a sinful desire. So, to eliminate a bad behavior, we must determine what the desire is behind it. Jesus said be holy, but he did not say we will never be tempted. The more we feed the temptation, however, the stronger it becomes. It's far better to pray it away, train your mind to not entertain it, and render it powerless early. Set whatever boundaries you need, communicate them clearly, and bring whatever you're struggling with to light so it doesn't have the opportunity to fester in your heart and grow bigger in the darkness. Temptation is going to happen, but you can still be holy. When it creeps in, rip up its invitation, declare truth, and find the help you need to overcome.

ENGAGING HEAVEN

Are you facing temptation today? What is your game plan to overcome it?

Things That Matter

"Whoever drinks of this water will thirst again,
but whoever drinks of the water
that I shall give him will never thirst.
But the water that I shall give him will become in him
a fountain of water springing up into everlasting life."
JOHN 4:13–14 NKJV

When we're serving God, he will put us in places that will blow our minds. All we need to do is get on our faces, repent, and follow him. But instead, we're constantly pursuing other things. Even great endeavors on our own terms and by our own accord will get in the way of what God can do through us if we would only surrender our lives to him. "If I could get this job…" or "If I just go into ministry…" or "If only I got accepted to this school…" There is nothing we're ever going to attain on our own that will completely satisfy. The only one who satisfies is Jesus. Honor God, seek his face, surrender your rights to his better way, and you'll have the best life ever. You'll never be in want for anything.

ENGAGING HEAVEN

Feed the poor, preach the gospel, minister to people, love your family, but do it with Jesus and under his direction. If you attempt any of these things in your own strength, they will fail to satisfy.

Place of Protection

When we live our lives within the shadow
of God Most High, our secret hiding place,
we will always be shielded from harm.
How then could evil prevail against us
or disease infect us?

PSALM 91:9–10 TPT

There's no such thing as a safety box in life. The way we avoid destruction is by staying close to the Lord and resting in that place of safety and peace. When we live submitted to God's plan and step into his presence, we'll be changed. Our desires change the closer we get to God. This isn't only regarding sinful thoughts but any worldly thoughts we may have as well. The more time we spend with him, the more we think like him, and the more heavenly-minded our desires become. Make room for the Lord in your heart and in your schedule. Although we have work or children or classes or whatever else we're busy with, ultimately, we're here to do kingdom work, and for that we need the presence of God in our lives. It may seem like drawing near to God is pressing closer to danger, closer to the fire, yet it's actually the safest place to be.

ENGAGING HEAVEN

*Where do you find refuge? From where do you draw
your strength?*

Living in Boxes

"You shall love the LORD your God with all your heart,
with all your soul, and with all your mind."

MATTHEW 22:37 NKJV

What fulfills us in life is not going to be what we've chased,
gained, or earned on our own. There are only two things
that bring true and lasting fulfillment. The first thing is our
relationship with Jesus, loving him with all our hearts. The
second thing is finding what we are called to do on this earth
and doing it. Whatever lie is having us believe that we can
find fulfillment elsewhere, we need to recognize, address, and
dispel it. It seems like as soon as we're born, we get thrown
into a box. We wake up in a home box, climb into our car box,
go to our office box, and learn how to live in a box. It's no
wonder we end up subconsciously putting God in a box. It's
time we got out of our boxes! Making a living is important but
not more important than making a life. So today, let's find out
what really brings fulfillment in our lives and run after that.

ENGAGING HEAVEN

*Go on a mission trip; go serve at a soup kitchen; go do
something out of your box to love people and serve God.*

Trust God, Not Feelings

Trust in the LORD with all your heart,
And lean not on your own understanding.
PROVERBS 3:5 NKJV

That word *all* is powerful. Sometimes we use controlling words like *all*, *every*, or *always* to push our point. For example, when we're arguing with our spouse, we might say things like, "You always do that!" In doing so, we're being moved by our feelings. But when the Bible says "all," it's a check we can cash. Our feelings are going to lie to us and change day-to-day. When God says "all" or "always," he means it. We truly can trust him with *all* our heart. He is our anchor whereas our feelings are as fickle as the wind. As followers of Christ, we live by truth and wisdom. Evangelist Smith Wigglesworth once said, "I am not moved by what I see. I am not moved by what I feel. I am moved by what I believe." We serve the Unchanging One, and if we give into feelings, we'll lose the blessing God has for us. We have to be people who are moved by what we believe.

ENGAGING HEAVEN

A loss doesn't change God, and sickness doesn't change God. He is always good all the time.

You Eat

You prepare a table before me
in the presence of my enemies;
You anoint my head with oil;
My cup runs over.
PSALM 23:5 NKJV

What do you do when enemies are all around you? You eat. God has prepared a table for you right in front of your enemies. Why? Because he's taking care of them, and you don't need to be concerned. So, relax, trust God, and eat up. The Bible is full of stories of people becoming so fearful, doubting, taking extreme measures, and running away, and in the end, God delivers them. And is it that much different in our world today? We stress and strain, trying to keep everything in our lives from falling apart, always feeling like we're living on the edge of total destruction, but in actuality, God has it all under control. We make life so complicated. Deuteronomy 20:4 says, "The LORD your God is He who goes with you, to fight for you against your enemies, to save you" (NKJV). So, when life is threatening to take you down and there are problems confronting you that are too big for you to handle, pull up a chair, rest, and trust God as he annihilates your enemies.

ENGAGING HEAVEN

Are you straining or sitting today? Are you fighting or feasting?

Jump over the Bush

What then shall we say to these things?
If God is for us, who can be against us?
ROMANS 8:31 NKJV

God has a race uniquely for you, and nobody else is going to run it. You are running a race that's been suited for your calling and gifting. God has a prize for you, and it's not only reserved in heaven for you one day. It's also for now. This whole goal of this life isn't to tap our heels like Dorothy from *The Wizard of Oz* and fly out of here. The Christian is invited to live in God's abundance here and now. But too many people just want to ignore or escape from their issues rather than overcome them. They want to be raptured from their roles of responsibility. They may see their issues as bigger than they are. But if you continually give things more power than they actually possess, your race is going to be difficult because every bush is going to make you stop. That's not an attack; that's what we call life. Jump over that bush and keep racing.

ENGAGING HEAVEN

God has miracle power and blessing intended for you now, and that should be your goal and expectation.

Soaking the Pot

"I will put My laws in their mind
and write them on their hearts;
and I will be their God,
and they shall be My people."
HEBREWS 8:10 NKJV

Have you ever left a dirty pot to sit overnight and then tried
to clean it the next day? Sometimes the food is so crusted on
the bottom that it takes twice the effort it would have if you'd
just cleaned it immediately. It's always better to deal with
stuff than to let it sit and harden. It also helps to soak the pot.
Soaking the pot in water helps to soften the food and makes
it easier to deal with. In the same way, we can soak our hearts
in God's cleansing water. That's the reason waking up early
and spending time praying, worshiping God, and reading
the Bible can change your entire day. Now, instead of being
scraped and scrubbed by the ups and downs of the day, your
heart is soft and prepared to be cleaned by God. It takes a lot
less effort, and you won't be nearly as tired by the end of it.

ENGAGING HEAVEN

*Is your heart hard and crusty? It might be time to go soak in
God's presence and love for a while.*

Clean Your Well

All at once, the woman left her water jar
and ran off to her village and told everyone.
JOHN 4:28 TPT

Isaac had to re-dig the wells of his father, Abraham (Genesis 26:18), because they had gotten filled with earth. Obviously, if a well is filled with earth, it's useless because it produces no water. So, if our wells become filled with the earth of this world and we can't tap into the living water of blessing, it may be time to dig some of that earth out. There is not room in our hearts for both the dirt of the world and the living water of God. It's vital that we routinely clean our wells so they remain pure and clean and life-giving. It used to be that water needed to be drawn every day, but we battle with a deeper, darker thirst. Jesus offers to satisfy this thirst once and for all. When the woman at the well encountered Jesus and understood what he was offering her, she left her water jug behind and ran into the city to tell everyone! He met a woman at a well, and *she* became a well.

ENGAGING HEAVEN

Are you thirsty for more than this world has to offer?

Harvest

"Why would you say,
'The harvest is another four months away'?
Look at all the people coming—now is harvest time!
Their hearts are like vast fields of ripened grain—
ready for a harvest."

JOHN 4:35 TPT

People want resurrection power, to know that God is real, and to see the gospel in action. The Lord has a harvest for us ripe and ready. Why are we waiting? What are we waiting for? The world is full of lost and hurting people *today*, and Jesus is on his throne *today*. Let's lift our eyes and recognize the need! We each have a place in it. We don't all have to become missionaries and move to the farthest reaches of the world. Praise God for those who do, but there are people desperate for the love of Christ in our own neighborhoods, at our jobs, even in our own families. There's no reason to wait four more months. Doors are open now, so what's keeping us from walking through them? Instead of falling into the carnal and mundane, let's dream again with God. Let's see miracles happen and lives transform. Let's step out of the mediocre into God's bountiful harvest.

ENGAGING HEAVEN

What is your role in the harvest? Who is God leading you to talk to or love on today?

Tend Your Garden

"The one sown among thorns
represents one who receives the message,
but all of life's busy distractions, his divided heart,
and his ambition for wealth result in suffocating
the kingdom message and it becomes fruitless."
MATTHEW 13:22 TPT

You weed your garden, right? By doing so, you're protecting the flowers or other plants you're growing. When it comes to our lives, the Lord may ask us to weed some things out of our hearts. We've all got weeds that we need to pull out so that the fruit God is growing in us and can continue to flourish. Some things just need to die. If God is going to bring you to greater levels in your life, then it's going to require some tending of your garden. This isn't just when you get saved. This is today. This is every day. What happens when you don't tend a garden regularly? The weeds take over, or the bugs move in. If you really want God to trust you with more, then get used to gardening on a regular basis and uprooting the things that don't belong in your heart.

ENGAGING HEAVEN

What weeds have gotten into your garden that you need to uproot?

Our Response to God

The Lord opened her heart
to heed the things spoken by Paul.
ACTS 16:14 NKJV

Every person is fearfully and wonderfully made. We each have giftings and callings and a unique way of seeing life. God has made us differently, and there is beauty in the Father having different children with different perspectives. But our lives are not going to be defined by our potential but rather by our response to God. He has been speaking, but are we listening? That's the only thing that matters. Our hearts have to be cultivated to receive what he is sowing. We have to be in a position to listen, grow, and learn. There's so much more about the Father that is going to be unveiled for those who want to understand and encounter him. That's exciting! But when our hearts are closed or our pride tells us we already know everything we need to know, how can God sow anything in our hearts? The soil is too hard.

ENGAGING HEAVEN

The Word is going out, but is it settling in your heart?

What Do You See?

The word of the LORD came to me, saying,
"Jeremiah, what do you see?"
JEREMIAH 1:11 NKJV

When you look in the mirror, what do you see? Is the first thing you see your flaws, or is it your beauty? Do you see a failing, shame-filled person, or do you see a mighty woman called by God and shining with his glory? The way you answer that question is indicative of the perspective you hold and will determine where you go in life. if you view yourself as not good enough and think God is frustrated with you, how can you believe the truth that God is completely enamored with you? You can't do what God has called you to do because you're stuck on your struggles instead of your strength. When you look at the world, what do you see? Do you see a hopeless humanity destined for hell, or do you see opportunity for God's light to go forth? In order to see things as they truly are, you need heaven's perspective. And that is only acquired through knowing God, reading his Word, and spending time with him.

ENGAGING HEAVEN

What do you see?

Because He's God

Whatever you do in word or deed,
do all in the name of the Lord Jesus,
giving thanks to God the Father through Him.

COLOSSIANS 3:17 NKJV

God wants to be a priority in our lives, not just today, not just Sunday, not just during special events, not just when we need something, but all the time because he's God. If God never does another thing for us again, he is still already worthy of all our praise. We still ought to love him and make him first in our lives. Even if he never heals another body or never touches another life, what he has done is already more than enough. Our faith can't be based on how things are going right now or whether God meets our timelines. He needs to be the priority of our lives regardless. The key to having God's abundant life is keeping him in his rightful place in our priorities.

ENGAGING HEAVEN

*Is God your priority? Is he the one you're thinking of?
Is he the one you're focused on?*

April

Separated unto God

As they ministered to the Lord and fasted,
the Holy Spirit said,
"Now separate to Me Barnabas and Saul
for the work to which I have called them."
ACTS 13:2 NKJV

The interesting thing about the Holy Spirit separating Barnabas and Saul for his work was that they were already doing his work. They were ministering and fasting, and yet God had something more specific for them to do. Some people are so desperate to be called by God that they attempt to separate themselves unto him, but it is the Holy Spirit who initiates true calling. We are all ministers of the gospel in our everyday life; we are all called to love, serve, pray, and proclaim the Word of God. Not everyone is called to the mission field or to a microphone. If we are, may it be because God is the one who set us apart and not because we are trying to prove ourselves to him or others. Let's go be ministers and commit ourselves to the works of God, and let's see where it takes each of us. But specific calling and separation come through a heart experience and an anointing. Trust God with that.

ENGAGING HEAVEN

Are you happy serving God where you are, or is he stirring something deeper in your heart?

Godly Wisdom

For the Lord gives wisdom;
from His mouth come knowledge and understanding.
Proverbs 2:6 NKJV

It takes an everyday commitment and constant attentiveness to not give in to the feelings and fears of our flesh. Even when we feel bombarded by negative emotions, we cannot allow those feelings to spoil the life God designed for us. Instead, let's choose to listen to godly wisdom. Fear's main goal is to convince us to believe a negative scenario that may never happen. "My husband is an hour late. He's probably cheating on me." "The bills are really piling up this month. We're going to lose it all." If you don't guard your mind from the doom and gloom narrative of the devil, your mouth will become his spokeswoman, and the negativity will spread. How can you praise God with the very same mouth that is spreading the enemy's lies and speaking death? The Word of God sets the agenda for life, not your fear or your feelings.

ENGAGING HEAVEN

When we're walking close with God, feelings are phenomenal. We feel God's presence when we worship and his encouragement and hope when we wake up and when we pray, but that isn't our measuring stick. God gives good feelings, true, but he is so much more than that.

Thankful

He had everyone sit down on the grass
and he then took the five loaves and two fish.
He looked up into heaven, gave thanks to God,
and broke the bread into pieces. He then gave it
to his disciples, who in turn gave it to the crowds.

MATTHEW 14:19 TPT

When Jesus was preaching, there were multitudes of hungry people, and they only had a little boy's lunch. Jesus asked Philip where they would buy enough food so everyone could eat, but he asked it to stretch Philip's faith because Jesus already knew what was going to happen (John 6:6). Philip started trying to calculate all the heads of people and the denarii needed, but he wasn't prepared for the miracle Jesus was about to do. See, we can get so much in our heads that we can't think clearly. We're never going to be ready for the wonders of God by counting heads and dollars. Jesus gave God thanks for the food they had, and that little lunch fed the multitudes with leftovers. Give thanks when you don't see the answer. When the answer comes and it's not what you wanted, give thanks even still. Give thanks in lack, knowing that your Father is going to come through.

ENGAGING HEAVEN

If you want breakthrough, write a list of one thousand things you're thankful for in the midst of the storm.

Vessels of Honor

"Whoever desires to become great among you,
let him be your servant."
MATTHEW 20:26 NKJV

If you always need approval from others, you're probably
not going to be great. Greatness doesn't seek approval.
Don't compromise your greatness in the court of public
opinion. Live what you believe. It's not a bad thing to
want to be great, but it requires certain things. One thing
greatness requires is teachability. Proverbs 1:7 says that
fools hate instruction. If we continually argue with wisdom,
how will we ever be great? We're either going to learn by
our mentors or by our mistakes. Which one would you
prefer? Another thing greatness requires is servanthood. The
disciples asked Jesus which of them was the greatest, and
Jesus' answer was that true greatness is displayed through
servanthood. He even demonstrated this principle to them
because, when everything was given to him, Jesus grabbed
a towel and washed the disciples' feet (John 13:3–5). Finally,
true greatness sees and encourages greatness in others.
Minimizing others does not maximize us. We're to be vessels
of honor, serving, blessing, and honoring others.

ENGAGING HEAVEN

*Can you be trusted with the flawed, human states of other
people? Can you help them through their thoughts and
emotions and steer them without judging them or beating
them up spiritually?*

Growing in Favor

Jesus increased in wisdom and stature,
and in favor with God and men.
LUKE 2:52 NKJV

Jesus grew in favor both with God and with man. Many of us grow in favor with man but not with God. The problems with that are evident. Many others, however, grow in favor with God but not with man. This disregards the importance of building solid relationships with others. The relationships we build are vital for our emotional, mental, and spiritual well-being—not just for us but for our families as well. We will find wisdom in our spiritual mothers and fathers in the faith. Those are the people whom we can draw from to help us shape our own lives and encourage us to seek God. We also need to be careful that we're not solely spending time with negative people who will squander our time and burden our faith. If they are who are leading us, we will eventually become as unhealthy as they are and get caught up in their bondage. Think about who's leading you and make sure you are growing in favor with both God and with others.

ENGAGING HEAVEN

Who is leading you?

Just Enough

I will take up the cup of salvation,
and call upon the name of the LORD.
PSALM 116:13 NKJV

In the Old Testament, the people would need to provide an animal sacrifice with just enough innocent blood to cover their sins and pay for forgiveness. This was an atonement because sin always has a price. The high priest would come, and he would dip his cup in water, and it was just enough to cleanse that person of her sins for the year. Old Testament salvation was temporary and "just enough." Sadly, many Christians today still settle for a cup of salvation, believing for just enough. It's time to break out of this mentality. We will miss out on all that God has for us if all we're doing is wandering around, trying to collect a little bit of water in our cups. That's the Old Testament way of thinking: it's hard and barely enough, we've got to make it happen on our own, we have to earn our own forgiveness. No. God doesn't want us to have a cup. He wants to put an entire well inside us, springing up with everlasting water! That's why Jesus came.

ENGAGING HEAVEN

Are you living with just enough, or are you walking out in the fullness of God's blessings?

Awareness Only

Having then gifts differing according to the grace
that is given to us, let us use them:
if prophecy, let us prophesy in proportion to our faith.
ROMANS 12:6 NKJV

It seems like today we are content with awareness only. We are aware of who Christ is, but do we really submit our lives to him? If we do not, evil is going to reign on this earth. God is looking for somebody to speak life, declare hope, and see the tide turn in this nation. The Bible says that we "prophesy in proportion to our faith." Our actions, then, show the level of our faith. A Christian who is loving and serving God with her whole heart is going to be speaking faith and hope and joy. She is not going to be crippled under the weight of the news and only prophesying doom and gloom. Just because we're in the midst of perilous times doesn't mean our faith level changes. We need to act on it but not react to it. We've been placed on this earth to make a difference, not to become caught up in the hype and fear.

ENGAGING HEAVEN

You are aware of what is going on. So, what are you going to do about it? Are you prophesying doom and gloom or hope and love?

Reputation

Let another man praise you,
and not your own mouth;
a stranger, and not your own lips.

PROVERBS 27:2 NKJV

There will always be people in life who want to cut you down, challenge your position, and tarnish your reputation. But if God is the one who lifted you up, placed you in that position, and declared who you are, then you have nothing to worry about. Instead of exhausting yourself by trying to prove your worth and defend against accusations, let your actions speak for themselves. Let your reputation as a righteous woman be proven by your track record rather than a retort. If nobody believes you and people unjustly think poorly of you, remember that your Father in heaven sees all and knows your heart. His opinion is the one that matters. In time, the truth always shines. Don't lose your focus or your effectiveness because you're so concerned about what other people think of you. Seek to please the Lord, and *he* will establish you.

ENGAGING HEAVEN

Has your character been questioned or your reputation dragged through the mud? How did Jesus respond to his accusers? How can you?

Two Types of Glasses

With all lowliness and gentleness, with longsuffering, bearing with one another in love, endeavoring to keep the unity of the Spirit in the bond of peace.

EPHESIANS 4:2-3 NKJV

By passing judgment on another person, we condemn ourselves because we judge from a position of arrogance and self-righteousness. Often, we habitually practice the very same things we denounce. Being offended, judgmental, and critical are not the fruits of the Spirit; they are not attributes of someone following the example of Christ. It is our natural position in life to be this way, but these actions do not represent the person Christ is transforming us into. Jesus even commanded in Matthew 7 that we aren't to concern ourselves with what's wrong with others when we have so much wrong with ourselves. And when we judge others, we're inadvertently setting ourselves up for judgment. There are two types of glasses through which we can choose to view life. We can either look at others through rose-colored glasses or a magnifying glass. Our selection will determine if we have peace, joy, breakthrough, and freedom or anger, bitterness, strife, conflict. Love those who are unlovely, forgive those who hurt you, and leave the judging to God.

ENGAGING HEAVEN

Which kind of glass are you looking through?

Miraculous Proof

Jesus answered and said to them,
"Go and tell John the things which you hear and see:
The blind see and the lame walk;
the lepers are cleansed and the deaf hear;
the dead are raised up and the poor have the gospel
preached to them."
MATTHEW 11:4–5 NKJV

John the Baptist was in prison, and he sent a couple of his disciples to ask his cousin, Jesus, "Are You the Coming One, or do we look for another?" (v. 3) Wait, what? Wasn't this the same guy who proclaimed, "I am 'The voice of one crying in the wilderness: "Make straight the way of the LORD"'" (John 1:23 NKJV), and now he is questioning Christ's authenticity? That sounds like some Christians today. If we're not careful, when times get tough, we forget the message that leads us through the good and bad times alike. Jesus' reply diffused all doubt, however. He didn't say, "Go tell John, yes, I am he." He told the disciples to give John a list of all the miracles that were happening by his command. Instead of defending his own identity, he allowed the evidence to speak for itself. If John had any doubt, Jesus had the proof.

ENGAGING HEAVEN

Do you see the proof in your life that God is at work and that he loves you?

Spiritual Olympics

As for us, we have all of these great witnesses
who encircle us like clouds.
So we must let go of every wound that has pierced us
and the sin we so easily fall into.
Then we will be able to run life's marathon race
with passion and determination,
for the path has been already marked out before us.

HEBREWS 12:1 TPT

Whatever you're striving for, training and preparation is mandatory for success, including becoming a spiritual champion. A fight in the ring that lasts a few seconds was preceded by a lot of hard work and diligence. Strength isn't developed overnight. God is preparing us for a race and for a reward. He rewards those who seek him diligently (Hebrews 11:6). The spiritual champion is the person sold out for Jesus, straining and training to become like him every day. If we're out of breath walking to the mailbox, we can't expect to run a marathon tomorrow. And if you struggle to have a daily devotional time with God, how do you expect to preach to multitudes? We don't become spiritual Olympians overnight; it requires diligence. So, start out walking and increase to a jog. The goal isn't perfection; it's to spread the love of Jesus.

ENGAGING HEAVEN

*God's not asking you to be just like Jesus immediately.
He's asking you to practice being like Jesus.*

Uncertain Times

Strength and honor are her clothing;
she shall rejoice in time to come.
PROVERBS 31:25 NKJV

We can't control when tragedy strikes, and we often don't understand why it does. Sometimes it's a big loss, and sometimes it's something smaller, like our car breaks down or we get a head cold. Either way, life happens. But how we respond to disappointments and tragedy determines our outcome. Our response will greatly influence where we end up in life. It's important that we take heart in the midst of uncertainty and remember that, whatever happens, God's goodness is unchanging. Instead of worrying about the future and about things we can't control, let's clothe ourselves in God's strength. Then we know for certain that we are equipped to handle whatever comes our way. We will rejoice in times to come rather than becoming overwhelmed and distraught. We live in a fallen world, and bad things are going to happen, but the Bible assures us that this world is not our final home. We're on a journey toward the one that is coming (Hebrews 13:14).

ENGAGING HEAVEN

How do you respond to uncertainty and disappointment?

God Is Your Provider

I am convinced that my God
will fully satisfy every need you have,
for I have seen the abundant riches of glory
revealed to me through Jesus Christ!
PHILIPPIANS 4:19 TPT

God is your provider. You may not know where your next paycheck is coming from, but God is your source. It's not the government. With all that's happening in the world today, it's best to allow the discomfort to push you closer to Jesus instead of deeper into fear. Let the devil's attempts to scare you drive you instead into the arms of the Father. In the midst of uncertainty, the Lord has something for you even more valuable than a paycheck: he has breakthrough and blessing and true prosperity. God has healing, signs and wonders, and peace waiting for those who put their trust in him. So, whatever you are facing, whatever insecurity you feel, this is the time to turn toward God, praying for and anticipating his provision.

ENGAGING HEAVEN

How have you seen God provide for you this week?

Create Your Space

"Refuse to worry about tomorrow,
but deal with each challenge that comes your way,
one day at a time. Tomorrow will take care of itself."
MATTHEW 6:34 TPT

We can't control every variable in life. And when we don't
feel like we have control, we start to spiral out of control
by attempting to control everything around us. We can't
become consumed by worrying about things that haven't
happened yet. We can't control things that are out of our
control. Instead, let's be good stewards of the things that
God has placed in our control. Some of those things include
choosing peace, joy, prayer, and forgiveness. We can choose
to read the Bible, love our neighbors, and worship God. It's
all about creating our space. What space are you creating? If
you want to live in peace, create an ideal space by prioritizing
God and your family. Don't blame distractions. Don't blame
your children or your church or the government. Decide that
in this season, you're going to create a space that's fruitful in
every way.

ENGAGING HEAVEN

*Have you created a space with the Lord and your family
that you love, or do you constantly feel the need to escape
your life?*

Discount Christianity

"Heaven's kingdom realm is also like a jewel merchant
in search of rare pearls.
When he discovered one very precious and exquisite pearl,
he immediately gave up all he had in exchange for it."

MATTHEW 13:45-46 TPT

Imagine a pearl so valuable, you'd be willing to sell everything to have it. That's what the kingdom of God is like. The merchant was on a journey to find something that valuable, and when he found it, he unmistakably knew it's worth. Have you recognized the worth of the kingdom? What are you willing to give up to obtain it? It's time for us to purchase our pearls of great price too. Serving God is going to cost you everything, but choosing to not serve God is going to cost you eternity. There's no such thing as discounted Christianity. The price for our salvation was already paid, and the cost was steep. Do you want to know the real God? Jehovah Jireh, the Lord of all power? Do you want to live right, think right, act right, and speak right? It comes with being in his presence and doing things his way. It's time we stand for truth and choose the hard, worthwhile way.

ENGAGING HEAVEN

What value have you placed on knowing God and being part of his kingdom?

Not Settling

"I will give you a new heart and put a new spirit within you;
I will take the heart of stone out your flesh and give you
a heart of flesh."

EZEKIEL 36:26 NKJV

We have to learn the difference between facts and truth.
Say a doctor diagnoses a disease that could cost someone
her life. That may be the fact, but the truth is our lives have
already been paid for. We shouldn't ignore facts, but we live
by truth. Nowadays facts and truth are so mixed up that we
can hardly distinguish one from the other. The waters are
so murky. People have lost their way and have forgotten to
listen to truth. What they think is holy is unholy, and what
they think is unholy is holy. We don't even know what's real
anymore because we don't have truth inside us, telling us the
difference. Being a Christian isn't summarized by showing up
at church or appearing to have life figured out. Being a real
Christian happens from the inside out. The facts of religion
want to change us from the outside in, but that's not how
true change works. The only way to experience real change
and to recognize truth is by knowing Jesus and inviting him
into our hearts.

ENGAGING HEAVEN

*Have you settled for the facts and for being a religion-based
Christian, or do you have the truth alive in you?*

Learning to Trust

"Listen to the truth I speak:
Whoever does not open their arms to receive God's kingdom
like a teachable child will never enter it."

MARK 10:15 TPT

We don't have to learn how to be critical; that's basically who we are. In fact, as adults, we have to learn how *not* to be so critical and how to trust more. On the other hand, we have to teach children how to be critical for their safety. We have to interrupt their perfect, innocent worldview to warn them about "stranger danger" and explain that some people are bad. When it comes to Jesus, he wants us to trust him with that innocent view of a child. Jesus wants us to rely on him the same way children rely on us. We never have to worry about tomorrow or doubt for a second that it's not going to work out because we know our Father has us and will take care of it all. We need to have that kind of innocence toward the Lord. We must trust. We must believe. We must love like children and see our innocence restored. He is working all things together for the good for us, and he has some great plans in mind.

ENGAGING HEAVEN

Are you ready to cast your cares on God, give him tomorrow, and trust that he knows what he's doing with your life? Can you approach God with the innocence of a child?

Acknowledge God

I will praise the name of God with a song,
And will magnify Him with thanksgiving.
PSALM 69:30 NKJV

So many people complain instead of acknowledging God.
It's easy to see all the things going wrong in life, but it takes
more intentionality to see all the things going right. We have
the choice to either acknowledge God in everything or just
complain. Even after God delivered them out of slavery,
lead them and protected them in the desert, and fed them
daily with manna from heaven, the Israelites continued to
complain. God was performing miracles right in front of
their eyes, but all they focused on were their problems.
We need to disconnect from critics and distance ourselves
from negative people who spend their lives complaining.
In time, they will pull us down as well. It's better for us
to acknowledge God, trust him to help us navigate the
problems, and thank him for all the blessings in our lives.

ENGAGING HEAVEN

*What are some of the things God has done in your life? Have
you acknowledged him regarding them?*

Little Foxes

You must catch the troubling foxes,
those sly little foxes that hinder our relationship.
For they raid our budding vineyard of love
To ruin what I've planted within you.
SONG OF SONGS 2:15 TPT

The Bible makes it clear that it's the little foxes that spoil the vine. Foxes are small and sneaky. Perhaps you have been guarding your heart from the big things: murder, adultery, and sins like that. But are you guarding your heart from the little things? Because it's the little, sneaky things that will really bring you down. It's your words, your attitudes, your thoughts. Over time, people become so bitter and offended that it destroys their lives. Do you think that happens overnight? Absolutely not. What happens is one little thought creeps in, then another little thought, then another, and before you know it, this thought monster is destroying your life and putting you in a bad place. The best way to beat this monster is to defeat sin while it's still small. Habits are much harder to cut off, so call sin out while it's small and chase all those little foxes out of your vineyard.

ENGAGING HEAVEN

*Have you allowed any little foxes to make their home
in your heart?*

Creating Mountains

> "I promise you, if you have faith inside of you
> no bigger than the size of a small mustard seed,
> you can say to this mountain,
> 'Move away from here and go over there,'
> and you will see it move!"
>
> MATTHEW 17:20 TPT

Romans 12:3 says we all have been given a deposit of faith. It doesn't matter how little—a mustard seed is like a speck, yet with faith the size of a speck, we can move mountains. Faith is that powerful. But with a speck of doubt, we're creating mountains. That's what is happening in so many people's lives today: they're not moving mountains; they're creating them with doubt and unbelief. It's so important that we feed our faith and starve our doubts. Starving our doubts does not mean running to the internet for encouragement or asking for advice from somebody who's not walking with God. It's easy to build a case for fear if we try to, but that is only going to lead to trouble. Fear is an insatiable monster that never quits. Fear desires to dominate and control us. God, on the other hand, wants to move mountains and perform miracles to feed our faith. It doesn't matter if the only faith we have is a speck the size of a mustard seed. It's time to take that speck and start speaking to every mountain blocking us from pursuing God and tell it to be moved.

ENGAGING HEAVEN

Are there mountains you have created in your mind?
Speak to them in faith today.

The Valley of Indecision

Elijah came to all the people, and said,
"How long will you falter between two opinions?
If the LORD is God, follow Him; but if Baal, follow him."
1 KINGS 18:21 NKJV

We can't live in faith and walk in fear. Either we bow before God, or we bow down to that spirit of fear that is in this earth right now. If we truly want to follow God, we need to choose faith over fear. When Jesus walked on earth, miracles happened. Now Jesus lives in us, and the ingredients for life itself are present, so why are we still worried? We are in the valley of indecision today: Are we going to trust God or allow fear to dominate us? God is not saying we won't ever feel fear but that we can trust him in the midst of fear. In Isaiah 43:2, he promises us, "When you pass through the waters, I will be with you; and through the rivers, they shall not overflow you. When you walk through the fire, you shall not be burned, nor shall the flame scorch you" (NKJV). Regardless of the threat, our God will be with us, so fear has no power over us.

ENGAGING HEAVEN

Are your decisions and lifestyle dictated by faith or fear?

Encountering God

Your words were found, and I ate them,
And Your word was to me the joy and rejoicing of my heart;
For I am called by Your name, O Lord God of hosts.
JEREMIAH 15:16 NKJV

Jacob worked himself into a really bad place by deceiving his brother, father, and eventually even his mother. There was a part of him that genuinely wanted the blessing of God, but he was trying to make it happen on his own instead of seeing God's face. There are people with pure motives who desire the things of God, but they turn to the arm of the flesh to make them happen, and things end up badly. We weren't ever supposed to live this Christian life without an encounter with our Creator. Christianity can't be limited to what's in our heads. And it doesn't matter whose daughter or wife or mentee you are. We each have to encounter God for ourselves. It didn't matter that Jacob was a descendant of Abraham and Isaac; he needed to meet the God of Jacob for himself. So today, let's lean into the grace of God, let's seek his face anew, and let's wait in eager expectation for what the Holy Spirit is doing in and around us.

ENGAGING HEAVEN

Do you want the blessings of God? Are you trying to make them happen on your own, or are you actively seeking fresh encounters with him?

Learning to Walk

He said, "Come."
And when Peter had come down out of the boat,
he walked on the water to go to Jesus.
MATTHEW 14:29 NKJV

What did Peter learn when he walked on water? As long as his eyes were on Jesus, he could walk. But the minute he looked down at the waves around him, he began to sink. We are not going to rise about the waves and walk toward Jesus if our eyes are on the world, if we're focused on somebody else's social media page, if we're filling our minds with bad television, or if we're worried about all the scary things happening in the world. We are not going to soar by living in fear of everyone else's opinion of us. God is working in us his miracle power, and he wants to call us to walk in safety through the storm. He is preparing us and stretching his hand out toward us. We can trust God's intentions toward us. Sometimes when we feel scared, vulnerable, and like we don't understand why things are happening, it's really the Lord teaching us to step out of the boat and walk toward him. We don't have to worry about the storm swirling around us because he's right there with us the entire time.

ENGAGING HEAVEN

When given a choice, many people will choose comfort over a challenge. What about you? Are you willing to step out of the boat?

Finding Your Voice

I thank you, God, for making me so mysteriously complex!
Everything you do is marvelously breathtaking.
It simply amazes me to think about it!
How thoroughly you know me, Lord!

PSALM 139:14 TPT

You're not wired like anybody else. You don't think, act, or speak like anyone else. Inside of you is a radical woman of God who, possibly, has been put down years ago. Well, it's time to restore who you truly are and get your voice back. God has given you a voice and a specific calling. What is it? You need to plug in to the reason why he put you on this earth. Many people never step out into their unique calling and specific voice because they're too insecure or unstable. They opt, instead, to mimic someone else's voice. Comparing yourself to others will be a death to your destiny. God has given you a voice, but whether you're using it is a different story. In a world full of echoes, God wants you to use your unique voice to share a specific message that he placed solely in you. This world needs to hear the voice God has given *you*.

ENGAGING HEAVEN

When you submit your gifts and talents to the Holy Spirit, he will put them to good use and create greatness in you.

Anna

You will seek Me and find Me,
when you search for Me with all your heart.
JEREMIAH 29:13 NKJV

Seeking first the kingdom doesn't mean just thinking about God and tithing; seeking first the kingdom means getting on our faces before the Lord. It means putting Jesus first in everything. When we arrive in heaven and crowns are handed out, they aren't going to just the preachers on stage. They're going to be given to women like Anna. Anna was an eighty-four-year-old widow "who did not depart from the temple, but served God with fastings and prayers night and day" (Luke 2:37 NKJV). She sought the Lord with her whole heart. Her whole life was dedicated to serving God. Even if we don't relocate and live at a church day and night, the point of our whole lives should be to serve God. In the midst of battle, David said, "One thing I have desired of the LORD, that will I seek" (Psalm 27:4 NKJV), and he was talking about God. God is looking for those who will shut out the world and seek his voice.

ENGAGING HEAVEN

Today, make Jesus the one thing, the only thing, and watch God breakthrough in your life in amazing ways.

Uncharted Paths

When He had called the people to Himself, with His disciples also, He said to them, "Whoever desires to come after Me, let him deny himself, and take up his cross, and follow Me."

MARK 8:34 NKJV

God wants to pull us out of the place of dependency on others and bring us through open doors. Excuses just comfort incapacity. "Oh, it's not my fault." "You don't understand the family I came from." When was the last time you challenged yourself? When was the last time you stretched yourself to change your routine? Because when you're not accessing the open doors God has for you, frustration and bitterness set in. You'll want to make excuses. You start thinking, *Well, maybe this isn't for me. It's not going to work out, and I don't want to risk failing.* See, the enemy of your soul wants to attack you. And when nothing changes in your life, you continue to follow the same passionless routine, you become an easy target. But there is so much more for you than dead patterns. Don't settle for "almost" when you're right on the brink of "amazing"! All it takes is a step of faith out of the norm and into God's unpredictable but completely reliable embrace.

ENGAGING HEAVEN

Believe God to see something different in your life. Reach out to someone, wake up earlier, spend time with God, trust him, embrace friendships.

Boundaries

Dedicate your children to God
and point them in the way that they should go,
and the values they've learned from you
will be with them for life.
PROVERBS 22:6 TPT

We don't go outside God's way of living and call it freedom. That's bondage. We set healthy boundaries for our children to keep them safe, but it is just as important that we set ourselves boundaries as well. When you don't set up boundaries in your life, you're the only one who gets hurt, but you're also the only one to blame. Boundaries are beautiful. They are the love lines of protection. It's hard to get anything done when you don't establish a line. This does not mean asking your flesh every day how you're feeling and drawing a line. It means being diligent and faithful to stick to the boundaries you and Jesus have decided on. Some days your flesh may not like it, but you need to be a person of your word, filled with integrity. It is imperative that we understand proper boundaries.

ENGAGING HEAVEN

Are you setting personal boundaries so you and Jesus can be together? What are they?

DIY Faith

Truth's shining light guides me in my choices and decisions; the revelation of your Word makes my pathway clear.

PSALM 119:105 TPT

The Bible is not a fairy tale or a comic book; it is a manual on how to live every day in this life. The Bible tells us that we've been given everything we need to live godly lives (2 Peter 1:3). That means whatever is broken in your life, there is a DIY manual to fix it: the Bible. It is our guidebook on how to navigate through our issues and overcome. If you're reading some self-help book as your spiritual guide, you'll be lost. If you're depending on the news to tell you how to live, it won't go well for you. Instead, rely on the Lord. The Holy Spirit is involved with you, fixing things in your life, and committed to leading you. God gave us the Bible to shine a light on our path as we navigate this dark world.

ENGAGING HEAVEN

Where are you lacking peace? Where are you missing joy? Where are you frustrated? What upsets you? What makes you feel downtrodden? Go directly to those areas, identify them, then go to the manual and find the solution.

Run the Race

Those who wait on the Lord
Shall renew their strength;
They shall mount up with wings like eagles,
They shall run and not be weary,
They shall walk and not faint.

Isaiah 40:31 NKJV

To run a race well, we don't walk through the track and just pick up speed at the end. In our Christian walk (or run), we need to be filled with the Holy Spirit and embrace that daily. If you met Jesus at a young age, great! Don't get off track or slow your pace. If you just met him recently, that is also wonderful. Grab your baton and get going. When your race is over, what are people going to remember? What did you stand for? Whom did you impact? What example have you passed down to future generations? At the end of your race, all that is going to matter is what was born into eternity through you. There is need all around us, so let's use our laps around the track to further the kingdom's cause and leave a lasting impact on other people's lives.

ENGAGING HEAVEN

How are you running these days?

He Is Here

"Fear not, for I am with you
Be not dismayed, for I am your God.
I will strengthen you,
Yes, I will help you,
I will uphold you with My righteous right hand."

ISAIAH 41:10 NKJV

In Matthew 14:22, Jesus sent the disciples in a boat to go before him to the other side of the sea while he went up a mountain to pray. The boat got caught in a storm and was tossed around by the waves and the wind. The disciples became so fearful, but Jesus went to them, walking on the sea. Many Christians today become fearful still. Don't believe that if you only had a certain amount of money or a new job or reached some other goal that you'd be fine. Fear doesn't respect boundaries. Fear wants to arrest your heart and steal the joy and the peace that God has for you today. The disciples were fearful because they were focused on the storm, but they should have been focused on Jesus. They should have realized that, even if he wasn't presently in the boat with them, he was always going to be with them.

ENGAGING HEAVEN

Instead of focusing on our storms today, let's remember that Jesus is still with us, protecting us, calming all our raging waves and winds.

May

Finishing Strong

Joseph took an oath from the children of Israel,
saying, "God will surely visit you,
and you shall carry up my bones from here."
GENESIS 50:25 NKJV

Joshua and Caleb saw the promised land. But there was someone else who made it too. See, when Joseph was on his deathbed, he made his children promise that they would carry his bones into the promised land and not bury him in the forsaken land they were currently dwelling in. Joseph fought for freedom. He knew they were one day going to break out of slavery. He believed God and held on to his promises. So, when it finally came time to enter the promised land, it was Caleb, Joshua, and a bag of Joseph's bones. There is something to be said for a man who held on to the promises of God even in his death. Let's be like Joseph. Let's be the ones to never give up, never doubt God's promises, and finish strong. God's promises are true, and they're for us today. Are you trusting him for them?

ENGAGING HEAVEN

Are you going after God's promises even if they take your entire life and into death?

He Lifts Your Head

You, O LORD, are a shield for me,
My glory and the One who lifts up my head.
PSALM 3:3 NKJV

God wants to lift your head. So many people live with their heads down, their spirits broken, but God wants to give confidence and faith and boldness to overcome. God wants to lead us to victory. There are Christians who walk in such confidence that it doesn't matter what happens to them. The card machine may say "declined," or the doctor may say "cancer," but they know who their Father is. He is the one who lifts their heads. They know that, in God, they lack nothing. Too many Christians walk around as if their spiritual bank accounts are in the negative, but God is in the business of forgiving debts and offering us spiritual shopping sprees. He wants to give us supernatural grace and breakthrough, but it needs to be a partnership. Let's take authority in our own lives and pray over our families and our circumstances. Let's lift our heads up and recognize that God is where our help comes from.

ENGAGING HEAVEN

If you are in a difficult season, you may need to start with small steps. Today, get out of bed, take a shower, go on a walk, and stand firm on the foundation that God has given you.

Touch of Faith

Jesus, immediately knowing in Himself
that power had gone out of Him,
turned around in the crowd and said,
"Who touched My clothes?"

MARK 5:30 NKJV

There was a woman who struggled with "a flow of blood"
issue for twelve years. Jesus was pressing through large
crowds of people, and the woman reached out and touched
him. Immediately, she felt in her body that she was healed,
and Jesus felt power go out of him. Jesus turned around
and asked, "Who touched My clothes?" (vv. 25–30). So
many people had been touching him and pushing up against
him, so Jesus' question makes me think that those closest
to him in the crowd were not touching him in faith. That
woman went and found Jesus, made her way through the
crowds, and reached out in faith to touch Jesus. The result:
she saw breakthrough and healing in her life. See, it's one
thing to know Jesus and walk alongside him. It is another to
truly believe in his power and deliverance and know that he
actually wants to move on our behalf. We must reach out for
Jesus with a touch of faith.

ENGAGING HEAVEN

*Read the whole story in Mark 5:25–34. Can you imagine how
this woman must have felt, both about being set free from
her ailment and about how Jesus responded to her?*

Thoughts Matter

For as he thinks in his heart, so is he.

PROVERB 23:7 NKJV

Our thoughts are powerful. So much of our lives are based on our thoughts. Perhaps we don't decide our futures per se, but we decide our thoughts, which form our habits; and our habits dictate our futures. Footpaths are created in our brains through habits, repetition, and cycles of behavior. Romans 12:2 warns us not to conform to the world's ways of doing things but to transform our lives, which takes intentionality— and that starts with our thought lives. What we think about matters. What we daydream about and envision has more of an impact on our lives than we may realize. That is why reading the Word of God and meditating on it in our hearts is so important. When we do so, we align our minds and hearts with the mind and heart of God. We become more like him and less like the world. Doing great things for God starts with thinking about the greatness of God. It doesn't happen overnight; it's a slow grind of clearing our minds, getting our hearts right, and creating healthy habits.

ENGAGING HEAVEN

Do you have any destructive thought patterns that you need to surrender to God and begin to rewrite?

Beauty

Your eyes will see the King in His beauty;
They will see the land that is very far off.
ISAIAH 33:17 NKJV

Don't let time take away your beauty. Don't let the rough season you're going through steal your fire. We're not talking about physical beauty but of having a beautiful heart that burns for the Lord. Not everyone stays beautiful. Many people start out on fire but end up in the flesh because the world and worries steal away their fire. There's something in you that's yearning for something deeper. That's obvious; otherwise, why would you be reading this book? Why would you care about engaging heaven? Decide today that you're not going to allow hurts from the church or other Christians to rob you of your beauty. Commit today to keep your heart warm and on fire and refuse to grow cold. Growing cold is the easy path because it deflects many hurts and pains, but that's not how Jesus lived. He opened himself up to love and loss, burning bright the entire time. Burn today greater than you ever have.

ENGAGING HEAVEN

What are you burning for today? Is it aligned with God's heart toward you?

Legacy

"Therefore know that the LORD your God,
He is God, the faithful God who keeps covenant
and mercy for a thousand generations with those
who love Him and keep His commandments."

DEUTERONOMY 7:9 NKJV

Legacy isn't just a final inheritance you leave somebody when you die. It's every single day serving God and putting the kingdom first in your life. When you look back, perhaps you've raised amazing kids and been an amazing wife, daughter, or friend. But true and lasting legacy happens when Christ has been the first focus. Fulfilled calling happens. It's not the inheritance or the house that are going to make a difference to your loved ones in light of eternity. It's when they witness you pray. It's when they watch Mom maintain composure in stressful situations. It's when your friends see an example of trusting God, praying for people when they're sick, and declaring life when something's hurting. The Bible says, "Train up a child in the way he should go" (Proverbs 22:6 NKJV), but you can't teach your children something you don't know or give them something you don't have. If you've not encountered God, don't expect to be able to teach your friends or neighbors how to become close to him. You have to set the example. God has a plan for you.

ENGAGING HEAVEN

Focus on heaven, focus on love, focus on life. You are going to change this world.

Increase

"No one can serve two masters;
for either he will hate the one and love the other,
or else he will be loyal to the one and despise the other.
You cannot serve God and mammon."

MATTHEW 6:24 NKJV

Jesus warns us that we shouldn't serve two masters—God
and money—and explains that the reason is because we
will end up loving one and hating the other. There's no in-
between. God wants to increase every area of your life, and
finances are part of your life, but our treasure should be
preserved in heaven—not on this earth. When Jesus came to
earth, he didn't come the way we thought he would. He came
through a virgin. The King of the world was born in a trough
used to feed animals. This is the Savior of humanity, the
"Lamb of God who takes away the sin of the world" (John
1:29 NKJV). It's a reminder to us that God's plan doesn't
often happen the way we expect. When we're going through
difficult times, we can remember that God's plan is to
increase us, but it's always from a heavenly perspective, not
an earthly one, and often not how we would expect.

ENGAGING HEAVEN

*What happens to our relationship with God when money,
foremost, drives and motivates us?*

Live on Purpose

Help us to remember that our days are numbered,
and help us to interpret our lives correctly.
PSALM 90:12 TPT

Why does it take trauma for us to contemplate the number of our days? Why is it that we begin to think about our purpose for life when we realize how fragile it is—like at a funeral or if we get a bleak diagnosis. Hebrews 9:27 reveals that "It is appointed for men to die once, but after this the judgment" (NKJV). We have limited, numbered days. This is not an upsetting thing. It is simply more reassurance that God has ordained us to be alive for a certain time and a certain reason. We are not on this earth to work a job and die. We are here to display the works of Christ, make him known, and shine his light wherever we go. We can't let other things number our days. Each one is held by the Father and given as a gift so we can walk in breakthrough and wisdom and revelation.

ENGAGING HEAVEN

Are you numbering your days, or is today just another day to you?

Counselors

Without counsel, plans go awry,
But in the multitude of counselors they are established.
PROVERBS 15:22 NKJV

Who is speaking into your life, sister? If you are the only one allowed to speak, you're going to encounter huge problems. If the only thing you eat is french fries, it will eventually kill you. And if you are only consuming the things of God that taste good to you, that will kill you spiritually. People can easily become isolated. Isolation is very scary because the Bible says when you isolate yourself, you destroy your sound judgment and only cater to your own needs (Proverbs 18:1). There's nobody in your life pushing you toward heaven. The Lord has surrounded us with people who are healthy and walking with God. Is there someone you can hug, touch, confide in, and rely on in real life? Not a computer screen. God has put people in your life whom you need, and there are others out there who need you.

ENGAGING HEAVEN

Paul said, "Follow my example, as I follow the example of Christ" (1 Corinthians 11:1 NIV). Who sets an example in your life worth following?

Waiting for Rachel

Now Jacob loved Rachel; so he said,
"I will serve you seven years
for Rachel your younger daughter."
Genesis 29:18 NKJV

The Bible says that Jacob loved Rachel, so he worked for seven years for her. Think about that. Some would have settled for Leah because, being the elder sister, marrying her would have been quicker and more convenient. But Jacob was faithful for seven years, and because of his great love for Rachel, it only felt like a few days (v. 20). Love should be powerful enough to wait for the right one. That's why marriage should not be a flippant or convenient decision. If seven days feels like seven years, you're in the wrong relationship. When you love God, service to him feels like an honor. It doesn't feel like it's a sacrifice. When you pray, when you dream, when you preach, when you witness to people at work, when you serve humanity, it needs to be done out of love. It's not a sacrifice.

ENGAGING HEAVEN

How does it feel to serve God? If it feels laborious instead of joyous, it may be time to take a step back and work on your relationship with God first.

Lasting Influence

"Let it shine brightly before others,
so that your commendable works
will shine as light upon them,
and then they will give their praise
to your Father in heaven."
MATTHEW 5:16 TPT

Think about all the people who have ever lived. God has never duplicated anybody. Every fingerprint is different, every strand of hair on your head he counts (Luke 12:7), so why are we so desperate to be like other people? Comparison is a trap. Everybody is known for different things, but because we live in this fishbowl world, we all look at other people's lives and want what they have, even though God has called us to something completely different. There's more to life than social media likes. Real influence is not entertainment influence or being popular. Is your life impacting others for good? Entertainers will die and be forgotten. Those who leave a true and lasting impact on other people's lives will be remembered. If we spent less time being jealous of the influence people have and more time contemplating the way God has wired us individually, we would most definitely leave a lasting and positive influence on this world for God.

ENGAGING HEAVEN

What influence do you have?
Who has eternally influenced you?

Bold as Lionesses

The wicked flee when no one pursues,
But the righteous are bold as a lion.
PROVERBS 28:1 NKJV

As a society, we cannot live in reaction to the world around us. It doesn't matter how influenced you've been by social media or how bitter you've become from the news. The Bible always has been and always will be greater than any worldly influence. It is our compass, our go-to, our solid ground. When society is shifting, we remain steadfast. What mountain are you ready to die on? Is it a societal or scriptural issue that drives you? We can't accomplish kingdom works if we're so stuck on trying to be politically correct and culturally relevant. There are spiritual concepts that have been around since the foundation of the earth. Perhaps society doesn't recognize them, but it's society that's constantly changing and refocusing, not the Bible. We have to change our mindsets to align with spiritual truths, not cultural trends.

ENGAGING HEAVEN

What are you willing to live and die for? What issues awaken your inner lioness?

Experience and Sight

"Blessed are those who hunger
and thirst for righteousness,
for they shall be filled."
MATTHEW 5:6 NKJV

The Bible was written by men and women who had a relationship with the Father, and it's meant to be interpreted by people who have a relationship with the Father. There are some Christians who think that since "faith comes by hearing," they can just play the audio reading of a Bible app and become super in the faith. But it doesn't happen because faith comes by continuously hearing and *listening*, not by just having heard. The lack of feeling spiritually full on the earth is directly connected to a lack of appetite. You can't run off the faith of anyone else—not your mother's, not your husband's, not your pastor's. It has to be your own. *You* individually must encounter Christ, and you must be hungry for him. Unbelief is far easier to catch than faith, but that will only lead to disappointment, hurt, and pain. However, when you encounter Jesus, the eyes of your faith become clearer and clearer, and your desire for righteousness will be filled.

ENGAGING HEAVEN

What does hunger compel you to do?

Life Is a Blink

Oh, satisfy us early with Your mercy,
That we may rejoice and be glad all our days!
PSALM 90:14 NKJV

We build this life with God, day by day, hour by hour, minute by minute. It's not the big thrills that make the difference. It's making wise decisions and taking steps in the right direction over time. One day we'll blink and realize we're so much stronger than we used to be. Let's not sabotage our days by taking them for granted. Each of us gets twenty-four hours a day, so we need to stay focused. Everything that goes on in our lives is ordained by God. He has allowed it. So, let's maximize it. Whatever conversation we find ourselves engaged in this week, whoever we are surrounded by, any surprise—good or bad—that comes our way, we have been already equipped to overcome. We can trust the process because we can trust that our loving Father is leading and guiding us. Let's follow him and enjoy life because one day we may blink, and it all will change.

ENGAGING HEAVEN

What are you doing today to follow God and make the most of this time given to you?

Attachments

Jesus said to him, "Let the dead bury their own dead,
but you go and preach the kingdom of God."
Luke 9:60 NKJV

Too many people believe that if they just get a husband
or if they just get a job, they'll be happy. They've become
attached to this idea that their happiness or self-worth is tied
to an earthly construct instead of to the one who created
their soul. Marriage doesn't heal a pornography addiction or
cure the ache of loneliness. Marriage doesn't heal the anger
in your heart from past abuse. Getting hired for a good
job, even getting hired at a church or a ministry, won't fix
your insecurities or your identity issues because you want
people to like you. The truth of the matter is our value isn't
connected to external things, and that's why becoming too
attached to anything external is dangerous. What we actually
need is another encounter with Jesus. Nothing else in our
lives holds the same power over us that the Lord who created
us holds. There is nothing else that can offer us fulfillment
because everything else is temporary and external. We will
only find it in the one who formed us perfectly for him.

ENGAGING HEAVEN

Are there any attachments you need to break off?

Jesus Requires Relationship

> "And then I will declare to them,
> 'I never knew you; depart from Me,
> you who practice lawlessness!'"
> MATTHEW 7:23 NKJV

Faith requires relationship. We can't talk to God once a week and expect to have an abundant life. We can't ignore Jesus for a month and then call upon his name only when we need his help. That's not how Christianity works, and it's not how relationships work. Think about how that would go over with a best friend or a spouse. Do you know how children spell love? T-I-M-E. Every meaningful relationship requires time, attention, and devotion. We've become too familiar with a God whom we barely even know. So, the two things we need to focus on if we want to live abundantly is deepening our relationship with the Lord and leading others to him through relationships with them. If we prioritize those two things, Christ's light is going to shine through us to the darkest places of the earth.

ENGAGING HEAVEN

Which meaningful relationships in your life do you need to prioritize more this week?

Mary Surrendered

"Great favor rests upon you, for you have believed
every word spoken to you from the Lord."
LUKE 1:45 TPT

An angel appeared to Mary and declared, "You will conceive
in your womb and bring forth a Son" (v. 31 NKJV). So, Mary
asked the obvious question, "How can this be, since I do not
know a man?" (v. 34 NKJV). The angel responded, "With God
nothing will be impossible" (v. 37 NKJV). Mary wisely and
humbly replied, "Behold the maidservant of the Lord! Let it
be to me according to your word" (v. 38 NKJV). Although
she must have known the stigma she would soon be facing,
Mary surrendered. Mary didn't have filters. She couldn't pick
the best selfie where her double chin wasn't showing. Her life
was open for everybody to witness and critique. And she was
judged. And she was condemned. See, there will be times in
your life when you will be highly favored in heaven but not
so much on earth. Mary realized that pretty quickly when she
was accused of being the mother of an illegitimate child, but
still she surrendered herself to God.

ENGAGING HEAVEN

*Surrender is not something we do only once when we
give our life to the Lord. Surrender is a position we hold
throughout our entire relationship with Jesus. How can you
surrender today?*

Faith like a Child

"Let the little children come to Me,
and do not forbid them;
for of such is the kingdom of heaven."
MATTHEW 19:14 NKJV

Greatness doesn't come in the level of your promotion;
it comes from the depth of your surrender. greatness is
established as we become more like children. Perhaps you've
been a Christian for thirty years and feel like you've reached
this level of spiritual maturity, but Jesus wants us to restore
the wonder of who he is in our hearts. He wants us to trust
him unwaveringly like a child again. When we face dangerous
circumstances, he never wants us to wonder if we're going
to be okay because we can know that he will always be there
for us. Children just trust that they're going to be taken care
of. They believe that everything is going to turn out all right.
We need to be a little more innocent, a little more trusting,
and a little more loving. Because if we're going to be great in
the kingdom of God, we need to be more like children.

ENGAGING HEAVEN

What childlike characteristics has God been working in you?

Hannah Contended

Hannah answered and said,
"No, my lord, I am a woman of sorrowful spirit.
I have drunk neither wine nor intoxicating drink,
but have poured out my soul before the Lord."

1 Samuel 1:15 NKJV

Hannah was barren. She was so overcome with sorrow that the priest thought she was drunk from the way she was acting. But Hannah answered that she had not had any alcohol. No, she was pouring her heart out to God. What do you do when you're frustrated? Whom do you complain to when you're struggling? Do you backbite and curse to your friends? Or do you pour your soul out to the Lord in grief? God wants you to be real with him and share your heart. That's what Hannah did. She didn't turn to her neighbor or her friend; she went to the Lord *first*. She was honest with him about her sorrow, and the Lord took her sadness and gave her a child (v. 20). Be like Hannah and pour your soul out to the Lord and watch him fill the barren areas in your life. God uses all of it by design.

ENGAGING HEAVEN

It's good to have close confidants but important to go to God first. What do you want to be honest with him about today?

Lessons from a Tree

The righteous shall flourish like a palm tree,
He shall grow like a cedar in Lebanon.
PSALM 92:12 NKJV

People have many fears in life. They chase things like political stability, financial stability, and familial stability, but few people today actually feel stable. The key to true stability is being rooted in God because he's the only one who will never change. When we're rooted in Christ, we are like solid oak trees; nothing can move us. We may sway under storms, but we'll never be moved. This is God's desire for us. Trees usually represent strength in the Bible. He wants us to flourish like palm trees and be strong like cedars, but that is only possible if we're holding on to Jesus and not depending on this shifting, unstable world. Business leaders, political leaders, and spiritual leaders are so often uprooted from their positions by moral or ethical failures. Maintaining integrity and remaining stable in a world that's ever changing is so important today.

ENGAGING HEAVEN

What are your roots planted in?

Framing Your World

"Open your mouth with a mighty decree;
I will fulfill it now, you'll see!
The words that you speak, so shall it be!"

Psalm 81:10 TPT

Proclaiming, declaring, asserting, all those things matter. We have a responsibility to frame our world. Think for a moment about the power of words. The Bible says, "Death and life are in the power of the tongue" (Proverbs 18:21 NKJV). Part of that sentiment we conceptually understand. If we're praying or speaking life or worshiping or decreeing the Word of the Lord, obviously that brings life. What we often don't understand is how the tongue carries the power of death. Our words are a weapon, and both the kingdom of darkness and the kingdom of light are waiting for us to use our mouths to benefit their cause. In many ways, we are the prophets of our own lives. Our words frame our world. Are we "can do" people or "can't do" people? Both declarations will end up being true. Nothing just happens. Are we using our words to tear down or build up? Are we speaking blessings or curses? Life or death?

ENGAGING HEAVEN

Take an account of your words today. Are they life or death?

Cranky Christians

"Do not sorrow,
for the Joy of the Lord is your strength."
Nehemiah 8:10 NKJV

Your level of joy is immediately connected to your level of forgiveness. When someone offends you, a contract of hurt and bitterness is placed before you by the enemy. If you sign that contract, you're consenting to a lease for a life of hell. Bitterness and offense are like weeds: they take root in your heart and destroy you from the inside out. When you walk with God, he fills you with peace. See, your level of joy is also immediately connected to your level of hope and strength in the Lord, which you receive by spending time with him. Peace, joy, and forgiveness are like guard rails on a bowling alley lane or shocks on a car. If your car has bad shocks, hitting a bump in the road can feel like hitting a brick wall. The same can be said for relationships. You don't just wake up one morning with marriage issues. You let your shocks get worn out. If your husband does something that really offends you, check in with God first and make sure your guard rails are in place.

ENGAGING HEAVEN

Cars require routine maintenance, and so do we. Are you easily offended? Have you been spending time with the Lord asking for patience and calm?

God's Original Recipe

"You shall not add to the word which I command you,
nor take from it, that you may keep the
commandments of the Lord your God which I command you."
DEUTERONOMY 4:2 NKJV

When we feel like there's turmoil or like things around us are a little unsettling, we become tempted to change the recipe. But God's recipe for life is time-tested and failproof. The Lord gave us the Bible: the perfect guidebook on how to live. Just because it's not always popular doesn't mean we can change the recipe. Truth is still truth no matter how we feel about it. When difficult times come, we don't move from the truth; we stand firm. It's almost like God is being slowly eliminated as this worldly form of Christianity creeps in. If you want to know what God wants to do, read his Word. The truth of God's Word is a message that's going to outlast time. Don't live a compromised life or compromise the message. What he promised, he will do. Every word he has ever spoken will come to pass. Do not lose heart. Even if you feel like you've been standing and you've done everything you can do, stay.

ENGAGING HEAVEN

Are you ever tempted to change the message of the gospel to fit your own needs or desires?

Isolation versus Accountability

A man who isolates himself seeks his own desire;
He rages against all wise judgment.

PROVERBS 18:1 NKJV

The Bible says two things concerning isolation: first, it will destroy your sound judgment, and second, you will start to do what's right in your own eyes. Both of those are dangerous. If there are no checks and balances and there is nobody else to measure from or check in with, how do you know what to look out for? In a place of isolation, how do you know if you're in right standing or even which way is up? Accountability is vital for a Christian's life. The devil wants to blur lines and confuse you. He wants to make what's unclean seem clean and what's wrong seem right. And you really can't have good discernment unless you're living in community with transparency. It is through being humble, seeking input and help from others, and constantly submitting our own will to the will of the Father that we will live in peace and maturity.

ENGAGING HEAVEN

Who have you invited to speak into your life?

Cracked Windshield

Deep calls unto deep at the noise of Your waterfalls;
All Your waves and billows have gone over me.
PSALM 42:7 NKJV

A cracked windshield typically happens accidentally. It only takes something small hitting it, like a pebble. You keep on driving, thinking everything is fine because it's not impeding your view. But before you realize it, the crack has spread across your windshield, and you're not seeing things as clearly as you once did. That's the danger with sin. If you don't take sin seriously, it will start to spread, overcome you, and blur your vision. Before you realize how big it has become, you cannot control it anymore. When the Bible says that "Deep calls unto deep," it means if there's a deep need in you crying out, then there is a deep presence that will respond. God hears and answers the deepest yearnings of our hearts, and this is how we go forward in the faith. Sin should deeply concern us, and we should desperately want to keep our hearts pure and our hands clean. If we do and if we cry out to him for help, he will most certainly answer and give us the help we need.

ENGAGING HEAVEN

Is there unattended sin in your life that you've grown accustomed to instead of surrendering it to God?

Much Ado about Nothing

When He came in, He said to them,
"Why make this commotion and weep?
The child is not dead, but sleeping."
MARK 5:39 NKJV

Jesus walked into a room where Jairus' twelve-year-old daughter had died. His response to everyone gathered was to ask why they were making such a loud ordeal. The KJV says, "Why make ye this ado, and weep?" Essentially, he said this was "much ado about nothing." What? It's important to understand that Jesus wasn't minimizing what was going on or downplaying the tragedy. But even in the darkest moments, we have to choose faith over fear. Jesus was reassuring them, "I'm here. I'm in the midst of you. As long as I'm in the room, death does not have the power; I do." Today, Jesus lives in us. If Jesus is flooding our hearts and our minds, fear cannot take hold. There's nothing fear can do when Christ is with us. It's not about minimizing tragedy, but by comparing it to God's power and goodness and authority, it's "much ado about nothing."

ENGAGING HEAVEN

Maybe you're weeping, frustrated, or fearful, but Jesus is whispering, "I'm not just in the room; I'm in you. You're going to be okay because I'm here." Do you feel the Lord with you?

Dad's Approval

Now, thus says the Lord, who created you, O Jacob,
And He who formed you, O Israel:
"Fear not, for I have redeemed you;
I have called you by your name;
You are Mine."

Isaiah 43:1 NKJV

Getting God's approval isn't work related; it's rest related. It's receiving who he is as your adoring Father. When you receive his love and affection, you have no reason to fear. And, you have no need to go searching for approval from others. The greatest revelation you can have is realizing how much God loves you, that he would give nations for you, that he gave his own life for you! Are you so desperate for a father-figure in your life that you compromise who you are? Does your apparel and your lifestyle show insecurity and a need for male affirmation? Or are you so confident in God's approval of you that you walk out as a self-assured, poised, unwavering woman of faith? It is impossible to fill the God-sized hole in our hearts with anything other than him—even our spouses cannot fill the void intended only for God. The strength and independence of God's daughters is beautiful.

ENGAGING HEAVEN

Does your lifestyle reflect that of a confident daughter of God?

Love Is Everything

He answered and said,
"'You shall love the Lord your God with all your heart,
with all your soul, with all your strength,
and with all your mind,' and 'your neighbor as yourself.'"
Luke 10:27 NKJV

It was Christ's love and compassion that burdened him to do what God led him to do. You're not going to do anything for God if there's not a fuel of compassion. There's dead religion that doesn't bring life, and then there's the spirit of the law, which is different. You have to be in touch with the heart of God to know it. See, the Word of God doesn't change, but the counsel of the Word is different from person to person. You might be called to be a missionary or a mother or a doctor—or sometimes all three! You don't get that kind of counsel without love, so check your motivation and make sure that love is rooted in everything you do. Make sure that you're giving your life to love people like Jesus did and that you're moved with compassion. Whatever you feel called to do on earth, no matter what it is, do it in a way that affects humanity with God's love. That is why you're here.

ENGAGING HEAVEN

Love is essential. It's the greatest commandment and the greatest gift. Are you receiving it? Are you giving it?

Handling Your Blessing

One thing I have desired of the LORD,
That will I seek:
That I may dwell in the house of the LORD
All the days of my life,
To behold the beauty of the LORD,
And to inquire in His temple.

PSALM 27:4 NKJV

People tend to fixate on something specific that they're desiring and believe their life would be okay if they could only have that one thing. They cry out to God, pray for the Lord to come through in a powerful way, seek his face day and night, fast, press in, get clean, and God answers their prayer. But then what happens? Do they continue to go to church, listen to God, and prioritize their time with him? Or are they suddenly too busy for "all that"? They give all, get all, then forget all. The very thing that made them great they quickly neglect as soon as they get what they want. So, what were they truly seeking: God or just his blessings? Don't worry about your problems; concern yourself with your connection with the Lord. When you seek God's face, climb higher, and reach new levels, your responsibility becomes greater, and your fall will be from a higher height if you decide to turn away from God.

ENGAGING HEAVEN

What do you want more than anything else?

New Thing

"Behold, I will do a new thing,
Now it shall spring forth;
Shall you not know it?"
ISAIAH 43:19 NKJV

Isaiah 43:19 is a powerful verse, but what does it mean when it says, "Shall you not know it?" God is warning us, "Make sure you don't miss it!" God is doing a new thing but not everybody is going to recognize it. That's intense. At the end of the day of Pentecost, there were two thousand people in the upper room, yet only one hundred and twenty were filled with the Holy Spirit. Where did the other one thousand eight hundred and eighty go? Home? There are no such things as rivers in the desert, but there are with God. There are no roads in the wilderness, but there are with God. He is opening new ways that we can't even imagine. Let's make sure we don't miss it.

ENGAGING HEAVEN

Read Isaiah 43 today and consider everything it says.

Feed Your Faith

To declare Your lovingkindness in the morning,
And Your faithfulness every night...
PSALM 92:2 NKJV

When you worship God, he grows bigger in your eyes, and your problems shrink. When you live without engaging heaven or focusing on what God has called you to do, life's problems seem bigger than your faith in God. That is why in a pure moment of worship, your heart focuses on God, and you believe that you can do anything—because he can. He seems bigger than your issues because he is. Feed your faith and starve your doubts to death. Engage heaven. Like an exercise program, do little things each day to work on your faith, and you will reach a point where you are surprised at how strong you are because of what God has done in you. That's how faith works. It doesn't happen overnight; it's a process. But when you commit yourself every day to feeding your faith, being close to God, getting your mind right, worshiping, reading God's Word, and counseling with the Father before you act in the flesh, your faith will build, and you will become stronger than you ever imagined.

ENGAGING HEAVEN

It's easy to tell who has exercised their faith and can handle pressure and who can't by what breaks them. Is your faith well fed?

June

Just Say No

> "But let your 'Yes' be 'Yes,' and your 'No,' 'No.'
> For whatever is more than these is from the evil one."
> MATTHEW 5:37 NKJV

Stress is killing so many people. Guilt is not far behind. In between those two extremes is one simple word: *No*. It's probably one of the hardest things to say. Why is it so hard to get that word out? We stay mad because we couldn't muster up a "no." We avoid certain people and events because we can't trust ourselves to say no. We worry, *What if I ruin the relationship?* or *Didn't Christ teach me to serve?* But God didn't call us to do *everything*. *No* is a powerful word because it establishes boundaries. If we can learn to just say no, it will keep us from wasting years of our lives trying to please others, it will allow us to preserve essential family time, and help us focus on what God is calling us to do. Don't say no to God...that's a bad idea. But with everyone else, know when to say no. If we truly live by our values, then most of our decisions will already be apparent.

ENGAGING HEAVEN

Don't ever feel compelled to fulfill someone else's dream for your life. Whether it's hobbies or businesses, people will always see you completely different from how God sees you.

Learning to Receive

"The LORD bless you and keep you;
The LORD make His face shine upon you,
And be gracious to you;
The LORD lift up His countenance upon you,
And give you peace."
NUMBERS 6:24–26 NKJV

God takes pleasure in the prosperity of your life. The word
prosperity can be easily taken out of context, but it means
he wants you blessed in spirit, soul, and body. The Lord takes
pleasure in you being completely blessed in every area of
your life, but for that to happen, you're going to have to learn
to receive. There's a posture of receiving. Jesus said of Mary
that she had "chosen that good part, which will not be taken
away from her" (Luke 10:42 NKJV). That means if you want
to do great things for God, and you want to see your life
transformed, position yourself to receive. It's hard to receive
when you're too busy talking and working and running
around, and that's why seeking the kingdom of God first
(Matthew 6:33) is so important. *First* means there's nothing
else before it; everything else in life is second. Being single-
minded is the key because nothing else comes before "first."

ENGAGING HEAVEN

Are you ready to make God first place in your heart?

Start Acting Childish

Jesus called a little one to his side and said to them,
"Learn this well: Unless you dramatically change your way of
thinking
and become teachable like a little child, you will never be
able to enter in."
MATTHEW 18:2-3 TPT

The disciples were arguing over who among them was the
greatest, and Jesus responded by saying one of the most
intense statements ever. He pulled a little child into the
middle of them and said, "Unless you change and become
like little Vanessa here, we will never even enter into all
that God has for you." See, the thing about children is they
aren't as intellectual because they're not fully developed
yet. They're only kids. But these little ones who don't have
it all together yet, who aren't full-grown, who haven't fully
matured...they're who we're supposed to become like. If you
want to be great, be like a child. "Stop being childish" may
sound insulting, but when it comes to faith, we need to start
acting more childish. Let's restore the wonder and innocence
of life and start trusting our Father the way children trust
their parents.

ENGAGING HEAVEN

*What are some qualities that children have that you'd like to
work on in your life?*

Finding Your Assignment

You formed my innermost being,
shaping my delicate inside and my intricate outside,
and wove them all together in my mother's womb.
PSALM 139:13 TPT

We each have an assignment from God, and if we don't
fulfill it, we're going to be miserable. People spend a lifetime
working to earn money, and by the end of it, they realize life
is empty because they're not living for any purpose greater
than finances. What are you called to do on this earth? What
is your assignment? He formed you in your mom's womb.
You were created for his purpose. What burdens your heart
so much that it stays with you? What makes you cry? David
asked, "Who is this uncircumcised Philistine?" when he heard
Goliath mocking God (1 Samuel 17:26 NKJV). As a young
boy, he realized his assignment was far greater than just
watching sheep. Nehemiah wept when he saw a city in ruins
(Nehemiah 1:3–4). He wasn't a builder, but he took on the
task of building a wall because his grief over the destruction
ignited a passion in him. That's how he found his assignment.

ENGAGING HEAVEN

*What grieves you? How can identifying that help you find
your assignment?*

Desolate Woman

"For more are the children of the desolate
Than the children of the married woman," says the LORD.
ISAIAH 54:1 NKJV

When you sing in the realm of faith, God fills you. It doesn't matter if you're barren or desolate, and it doesn't matter if you feel empty or alone. God will fill your faith when you ask him to do so. This means God wants to fill with his goodness and love every area in your life that is barren. He's going to turn your biggest area of pain into your greatest testimony if you'll give him your brokenness and sing out about his goodness. The biggest area of pain in your life will be what produces the most fruit. Like the story in the Bible of the Shunammite woman who made room for the prophet to stay (see 2 Kings 4), make room for God in your heart. Like her, you will receive blessing and end up blessing your whole household when you make room for God in anticipation for what he is going to do.

ENGAGING HEAVEN

Read 2 Kings 4:8–37. What lessons for your own life can you draw from the faith of the Shunammite woman?

Being Available

"And to one he gave five talents,
to another two, and to another one,
to each according to his own ability;
and immediately he went on a journey."

MATTHEW 25:15 NKJV

Every time the Holy Spirit nudges us to do something and we don't listen, we desensitize ourselves to his voice. In time, our hearts grow cold. We can't continually say no to God and expect to live an abundant life. If we're so busy running our own schedules and agendas that we're no longer sensitive to the Holy Spirit's nudging, we'll never truly live in the full abundance that God intends for us. See, it's not about your ability...it's about your availability. God gave everyone a talent. Ultimately, the question is what is your availability to use the talent he gave you? That's what is going to determine what you do. The question isn't whether you have talents, because you have them. The question is: What are you doing with what he has given you?

ENGAGING HEAVEN

Are you so busy making a life that you are no longer truly living? Are you taking time to listen and investing in the talents God has given to you?

False Expectations

"Look at the birds of the air,
for they neither sow nor reap nor gather into barns;
yet your heavenly Father feeds them.
Are you not of more value than they?"

MATTHEW 6:26 NKJV

We all have to deal with the expectations we had of life versus the reality we actually live in. Those expectations are going to be far more difficult if we allow the world to set our worth instead of finding out who we are according to God. The world can't tell us what we're worth, and it cannot dictate what we're called to do. Only God can do that. When we're faced with the temptation to look perfect or seem super spiritual and we write tweets and post comments to build our self-esteem, what we're really doing is setting our worth by a standard that isn't real. Is your worth determined by the "likes" you get? Is your peace determined by your financial stability? What we should be doing is seeking the kingdom of God first because all the other things will be added after that (v. 33). Don't worry. Just keep your focus in the right place.

ENGAGING HEAVEN

How can you recognize false expectations and set godly ones for yourself?

Complaining Corrupts

A joyful, cheerful heart brings healing to both body and soul.
But the one whose heart is crushed
struggles with sickness and depression.

PROVERBS 17:22 TPT

Complaining is the worst possible thing you could do for your spiritual health. It is toxic and will corrupt every area of your life. As a daughter of God, there is no room for that garbage in your heart. That's why God tells us to dwell on the positive things (Philippians 4:8). When you complain, your mind shifts to focusing on what's wrong in your life rather than how your life is blessed. Further, you distract and bring down those you are complaining to. Many of the things happening in your life are a result of your words, both good and bad, because what you focus on expands. So, if you keep thinking no one loves you, no one understands you, you're misunderstood, and so forth, that's what you're going to see more of. But if you focus, instead, on the wisdom of Philippians 4:8 and dwell on pure, lovely, virtuous things, you will see your life turn around into a beautiful portrayal of something much more praiseworthy.

ENGAGING HEAVEN

When you feel the urge to complain, what true and noble things can you call to mind instead?

Moderation

Whoever has no rule over his own spirit
Is like a city broken down, without walls.
PROVERBS 25:28 NKJV

The Bible says, "For the love of money is a root of all kinds of evil" (1 Timothy 6:10 NKJV). Money is not the problem; what we do with it is. The same could be said about our time or our stuff—like our devices. Are we using what we have for good or evil? Are we moderating them? Because in moderation, all these things have the potential to be wonderful blessings. But if we are not careful, they will destroy us. We need to get back to focusing on God and making room for him because whatever you make room for in your life is going to overtake you. Take a hard inventory. Look over your heart. Search your life. Matthew 6:6 says, "When you pray, go into your room, and when you have shut your door, pray to your Father who is in the secret place" (NKJV). God has a secret place waiting for you. There is an inner room where God wants to take you so that you can spend undistracted time with him.

ENGAGING HEAVEN

What areas in your life do you need to moderate better? Where does your time go? Where does your money go?

White Hot Fire

He will submerge you into union with the
Spirit of Holiness and with a raging fire!

Matthew 3:11 TPT

On the day of Pentecost, tongues of fire fell on the
individuals present (Act 2:3). Fire fueled the early church. It
empowered the disciples. The Bible says that "our God is a
consuming fire" (Hebrews 12:29 NKJV). If our God is a God
of fire and burning and passion, then why aren't we on fire as
well? Our nation has a God-sized hole in it that only the Holy
Spirit can fill, and he's going to fill it by using believers who
are burning for God. Cold Christians and dead religion will
not accomplish anything. The Lord is looking for people who
are white hot for him, burning for the things he wants to do.
Jesus didn't die on the cross just so we could go to church.
He created us to walk in fire and power. True believers
burning for God have always been a precursor to great things
happening.

ENGAGING HEAVEN

What sets your heart on fire?

Ignoring Waves

He stood and rebuked the storm, saying, "Be still!"
And instantly it became perfectly calm.
MATTHEW 8:26 TPT

We all have the same Jesus, and he has overcome the world.
The story of our lives is not about storms or dark times.
It's about Jesus and how he helped us overcome. We can't
focus too much on the waves because, like the storms we
go through, all of it is about Jesus. He's the focal point...the
punch line...the great reveal. We have an enemy who is after
us, and we can't control what goes on around our ship, but
we can control who the anchor of our soul is. We will most
definitely be met with resistance at times, but Jesus is our
peace and our power. Our life stories are not about the wind
and the waves, about how low we've been or the dark days
we've endured. Our stories are about how Jesus calms the
storms and has all the power. He deserves the glory. Don't
give the spotlight to darkness...give it to him.

ENGAGING HEAVEN

What has been the story of your life up to this point?

Culture of Wisdom

Wisdom calls aloud outside;
She raises her voice in the open squares.
PROVERBS 1:20 NKJV

Wisdom is referred to as "her" in the Bible. Proverbs 14:1 says, "The wise woman builds her house, but the foolish pulls it down with her hands" (NKJV). So, how can you create a culture of wisdom instead of foolishness in your household? Job 28:28 explains that "the fear of the Lord, that is wisdom, and to depart from evil is understanding" (NKJV). What do you fear more: The Lord or those upcoming bills? When was the last time you got up and walked away from evil? You are an example to your family. You can touch heaven for your family and for your lineage and know that, when you die, this earth was changed because of you. I charge you to leave a legacy, a spiritual legacy of wisdom, for your household. There are more valuable things than just the accumulation of physical wealth that you can pass on. Choose wisdom, trust God, be the best version of you, and God will do the rest.

ENGAGING HEAVEN

Read Proverbs 31. How can this woman's endeavors and faith correlate with our modern lifestyles?

Four Spirits

The LORD showed me four craftsmen.
And I said, "What are these coming to do?"
ZECHARIAH 1:20-21 NKJV

An angel showed Zechariah four horns, which represented four spirits who were up to no good; they were tormenting spirits (v. 19). Now, right before this vision, God revealed that he was jealous for Jerusalem. He said he was going to bring prosperity to his cities (v. 17). These four spirits had come, and no one could lift their head up because they were so dismayed and tormented. But the angel revealed that "craftsmen" were coming to terrify these spirits. And who was the greatest craftsman to ever live? Who lifted the heads of the downcast and freed people from spiritual torment? The carpenter Jesus Christ. He is the master builder. He is the lifter of our heads (Psalm 3:3) and the Savior of our souls. The enemy is oppressing too many people with the spirit of depression and holding their heads down, but the spirit of the carpenter will lift our heads, build us back up, and show us greater things than we could possibly imagine.

ENGAGING HEAVEN

Are you ready to pick your head back up? You don't have to do it alone. Jesus is ready to help you.

Living Empty

He said, "Go, borrow vessels from everywhere,
from all your neighbors—empty vessels;
do not gather just a few."
2 KINGS 4:3 NKJV

There was once a poor widow who cried out to Elisha, "The creditor is coming to take my two sons to be his slaves" (v. 1 NKJV). He asked her what she owned in her house, and she admitted the only thing she had was a jar of oil. So, he sent her out to find all the empty vessels she could, and when she poured the oil into the vessels, it was enough to fill all of them and was more than enough to pay off her debt. Now, Elisha didn't tell her to find silver or gold vessels. He simply told her to find *empty* vessels. They needed to be empty so God could fill them. That was the only qualification. In the same way, God wants us to go to him empty and ready to be filled. When we approach God full of other things, without feeling any need or hunger, how can God pour into us? The more we empty ourselves, the more God can fill us up.

ENGAGING HEAVEN

Can you imagine going to a buffet of the finest foods when you are already full of cheap food? Are you filling yourself with cheap, temporary things rather than God's lasting love?

Faith Reps

"But the ones that fell on the good ground are those who, having heard the word with a noble and good heart, keep it and bear fruit with patience."

Luke 8:15 NKJV

Have you ever faced a one-hundred-pound problem, but you only had fifteen pounds of faith? We can't sit around and hope that God will sprinkle magic dust on us to make us strong. We have work to do. There's no quick solution, no elevator to the top. Faith is like a muscle that we have to exercise. It takes hard work, diligent prayer, faithfulness, and saying no to some things we want to say yes to. If we're not exercising our faith muscle, it's not going to grow. And how do we expect to be strong enough to move mountains with flabby faith? God can guarantee his end of the deal, but he never guaranteed our potential. He gave us everything we need to grow strong in the faith, but we still have to put in the time. Let's commit to doing our daily faith reps. Let's be the kind of Christians who actually read the Bible, who listen to the voice of God, who step out of our comfort zones, and who see mountains move.

ENGAGING HEAVEN

What steps will you take today to build your faith?

Poverty Mindset

"Why do you spend money for what is not bread,
And your wages for what does not satisfy?"
Isaiah 55:2 NKJV

Poverty is not only financial. It is also a mindset, and it shows up in many different forms: it makes you think you're not good enough, that you'll never accomplish what is in your heart to do, maybe that you're not very smart. You may have absorbed lies others have told you about yourself since childhood. Whatever deficit is manifesting in your life, keeping you from living for the purposes of God, is a poverty mindset. Often when people have a deficit mindset, they start to blame others. It's always everybody else's fault. But faith doesn't blame everybody else; it takes responsibility and believes in God to overcome. Another sign of a poverty mindset is always trying to justify things. People justify their situations by claiming they don't actually care, or maybe they justify being broke by saying they're too spiritual for money. Poverty isn't a financial amount. The religious spirit is a withholding spirit. We need to rise above and be people who are diligent, aware, armed, and engaged.

ENGAGING HEAVEN

Do you see any signs of a poverty mindset in yourself? How can you call them out and address them?

Created for Praise

Now when they began to sing and to praise,
the LORD set ambushes against the people of Ammon,
Moab, and Mount Seir, who had come against Judah;
and they were defeated.

2 CHRONICLES 20:22 NKJV

When we worship, things change. There's great warfare, even weaponry, found in praise. We were created to praise and worship the Lord; it's in our DNA. It's one of the reasons we're here on this wonderful planet. Second Chronicles 20:22 offers us insight to God's heartbeat behind praise. Because the assembly of Judah and Jerusalem praised God, because their priority and focus was him, God defeated their enemies for them. Do you have enemies or problems in your life? The first step to defeating them is to prioritize praise. Protect your time with the Lord. Paul and Silas were in prison praying and singing hymns. Now, prison isn't the most ideal circumstance, but they chose to use that time to worship God. In response, while they were worshiping, God sent an earthquake that opened the prison doors and broke off their chains (Acts 16:25–26). Whatever prison you feel trapped in, whatever chains you feel are holding you back, your greatest way to escape is to stop struggling and start worshiping. Praising God opens doors too heavy for us to move.

ENGAGING HEAVEN

Spend this week focused on praising God instead of focusing on your problems.

Heartsick

Hope deferred makes the heart sick,
But when the desire comes, it is a tree of life.
PROVERBS 13:12 NKJV

There are a lot of heartsick people today. They are not living their dreams and not feeling fulfilled. The Bible compares fulfilled desire to a tree of life because when we realize and remember our calling and when we're seeing that calling being fulfilled, it brings us to a place of hope and growth. So, let's spend more energy and effort on realizing the desires God has for us and those he has put in our hearts than we do dwelling on what's not happening for us in life. What Scriptures are we holding on to? Job 8:7 says that where we begin in life will seem unimportant because our futures will be so successful. Jeremiah 1:5 reveals that before we were even in the womb, God ordained us. Jeremiah 29:11 lets us know that God has good plans for us. We need the joy of the Lord to be restored in us again.

ENGAGING HEAVEN

What encouraging Scripture verse will you focus on this week as you search out and work on fulfilling the calling God has placed in your heart?

Birthing Air

We have been with child, we have been in pain;
We have, as it were, brought forth wind.
ISAIAH 26:18 NKJV

What the Lord was explaining in Isaiah 26:18 was that Israel claimed to be pregnant, but when it came time to deliver, they only brought forth wind. God was rebuking them, saying, "Look, what you're saying is one thing, but what you're doing is another." Many people want to be in ministry, but they don't take the time to submit their intentions to God or to other wise friends. They don't spend time studying or praying or learning. God wants us to be pregnant with real substance and not carry around whatever crazy dream we birthed ourselves that wasn't given or blessed by him. God absolutely wants us to be people of faith...but also people of substance. Get filled, get pregnant with the purposes of God. Be diligent with those purposes, and your life will turn around. Then, when it comes time to deliver, instead of just blowing wind, you will bring forth life.

ENGAGING HEAVEN

What has God birthed in you?

Last Words

"Go therefore and make disciples of all the nation,
baptizing them in the name of the Father
and of the Son and of the Holy Spirit,
teaching them to observe all things
that I have commanded you."
MATTHEW 28:19-20 NKJV

It is so easy to become focused on this temporary world since it is what surrounds us all day long. Likewise, it is so easy to get distracted from the true mission God has called us to do. We are so in love with this earth, but the reality is, we are only passing through. This place should never feel exactly right because it is not the world we were ultimately created for. What is life worth? What are we here for? We are here to do the works of Jesus; to finish what was started that day with his last words. Our mission was and still is to preach the gospel. Truth doesn't look for culture to back it up. Miracle power is still available on the earth today and the Lord is looking for people who will stand on his Word and believe it. The Holy Ghost in us is ready to do the great works Jesus has called us to do, and we shouldn't put limitations on what he wants to accomplish through us.

ENGAGING HEAVEN

We are at a turning point in this nation, and the only thing that is going to change it is the power of the Holy Spirit. When you choose to do his will, boldness will come upon you.

Drawing Wisdom

A fool is in love with his own opinion,
but wisdom means being teachable.
Proverbs 12:15 TPT

God can do anything. God could give us wisdom from anywhere, but he often chooses to offer wisdom through other people who have gone before us and learned many lessons already. If you are going through a difficult season, have you thought about reaching out to someone wiser than you? Are you thirsty for wisdom? Are you hungry for more understanding and growth? If so, it is often going to lead you to other people. You're being led by something. Unfortunately, it could be the media. But if you're willing to listen, learn, and submit your heart to somebody who has experienced greater breakthrough than you, there's so much more waiting for you. In your search for wisdom, study the Scriptures, pray to God, and invite other people to speak into your life and share their experiences.

ENGAGING HEAVEN

Whom has God put around you? Whom are you drawing wisdom from? Whom do you need to stop drawing from?

Lack of Revelation

When there is no clear prophetic vision,
people quickly wander astray.
But when you follow the revelation of the Word,
heaven's bliss fills your soul.
PROVERBS 29:18 TPT

What you behold, you become. So, what's your vision? It's
going to take faith and vision to declare that God is moving
on your behalf and to believe that your breakthrough is
around the corner. It's going to take faith to stand on God's
promises, to lean on the Word of God, and to understand the
revelation of Christ. There were two trees in the garden that
represented choice, and in your life today, there are still two
trees. Which one will you choose? Everything you're facing
offers two potential narratives. Are you going to listen to the
lies of hell or the report of the Lord? The devil wants you to
give up, to quit, to cast off restraint and become unhappy.
But when you listen to the Lord, he will rebuild your faith,
and you will realize that he is your provider, your healer, your
mentor, and your everything.

ENGAGING HEAVEN

*What is God revealing to you the more you read his Word
and spend time with him?*

Embrace Breaking

So Jacob called the name of the place Peniel:
"For I have seen God face to face,
and my life is preserved."
GENESIS 32:30 NKJV

God met and wrestled with Jacob and disjointed his hip, and this all happened at a place called Jabbok, which means "the place of breaking." But this place of breaking ended up being his place of blessing, which is so often how it goes. Moses was in the desert and experienced great loss. Job was broken and had everything taken from him. Joseph spent fourteen years in prison, and Paul also spent time in a prison, broken. But it was in that breaking where their blessing came. God can heal every area in your heart that has been hurt or broken. It's time we start to embrace breaking instead of running from anything that's challenging. Rather than wondering where God is or why hard things are happening to you, ask if it could be that God is allowing some things in your life to mold you and make you, to prepare you for what he has called you to do.

ENGAGING HEAVEN

Could it be that God is perfecting his plan through you as you experience some of your current struggles?

Useless Polished Rocks

"His lord said to him, 'Well done, good and faithful servant;
you have been faithful over a few things,
I will make you ruler over many things.'"

MATTHEW 25:23 NKJV

In the parable of the talents, the master gave to each
according to his own ability. God already has a recognition
of what we can handle and manage. Jesus was using this
parable to explain to the disciples, and to us, that life is not
about what's fair; it's about being faithful with our share. We
are stewards of life. We are stewards of our family, finances,
and the mysteries of the kingdom. What we have been
given was not meant to be hidden away; it was intended for
investment. We're to invest our time, money, talents, and
love into other people. The servant who was only given one
talent went religious. All he wanted to do was protect and
preserve what was his and not try to advance the kingdom at
all. He hid it under a rock. Perhaps he thought he was doing
the master a favor by polishing it every day, but what does
God care about polished rocks? He wants good stewards. He
wants a return on his investments. He wants us to be bold,
not to hide.

ENGAGING HEAVEN

How are you investing what God has given you?

Double Trouble

"Return to the stronghold,
You prisoners of hope.
Even today I declare
That I will restore double to you."
ZECHARIAH 9:12 NKJV

A lot of people live hopelessly. The Bible says, "Hope deferred makes the heart sick" (Proverbs 13:12 NKJV). Something happens when promises aren't fulfilled when or how you thought they would be. Maybe you feel like God didn't meet your expectations, so your trust is challenged. If you're not careful, sickness sets in. Sickness of the heart is worse than physical sickness because sickness of the heart will disqualify you from what God has called you to do. It will cause you to become bitter, angry, offended, hurt, and feel rejected. It leaves you in a pit of fear and anxiety. Looking around at this world, if there's anything we need today, it's biblical hope. Hope is what changes circumstances because hope is what gives you the confidence and encouragement to make a change. Every time the Bible talks about hope, it's like a joyful anticipation of good things. Elijah got a double portion. Job lost everything and was restored double. Solomon's temple was rebuilt twice; it was double restoration.

ENGAGING HEAVEN

What if every time you faced a difficulty, felt disappointed, or things didn't work out, you receive double?

It's Written on Your Face

Everyone admires a wise, sensible person,
but the treacherous walk on the path of ruin.
PROVERBS 13:15 TPT

If cabin pressure drops too low on an airplane, the oxygen masks release. Do you know why you put your own mask on first before you help anyone else? Because if you pass out from a lack of oxygen, you can't help anybody else. So many people, mothers especially, are so busy trying to help everyone else with their masks, all the while they can't breathe. In life, they are passing out due to exhaustion and being spiritually burned out. They're so busy serving and working and taking care of the kids that they've lost their identity. They forgot themselves. Dear tired mother, you're not going to be any help to anyone if you're not strong inside. You can see on a person's face if she is happy, upset, or hurting. Your inner destruction will be evident on your face, so make sure you take time for yourself and strengthen yourself in Jesus—and put on your happy face.

ENGAGING HEAVEN

Are you walking wisely and sensibly? Or are you harboring internal destruction that you need to deal with first before you can help others?

Different Seasons

To everything there is a season,
A time for every purpose under heaven.
ECCLESIASTES 3:1 NKJV

There are different seasons for different things. There is an appropriate time for mourning and for rejoicing. The day and the night repeat every twenty-four hours. Genesis 8:22 says, "While the earth remains, seedtime and harvest, cold and heat, winter and summer, and day and night shall not cease" (NKJV). Seed isn't in question. Neither is harvest. The question is time. What are you doing with your time? What has God called you to in this season? Older women who have been through life can impart a lot of their wisdom into younger women. Younger women have the perfect opportunity to exemplify humility and learn from older women. Married women have an unparalleled opportunity to demonstrate their love and service to God by loving and serving their families. Single women are in a perfect position to love God through the way they use their time to serve him and others. God has created different seasons for different reasons. All of them are beautiful in their own way.

ENGAGING HEAVEN

What season are you in, and what is beautiful about it?

Fruit

"Out of the virtue stored in their hearts,
good and upright people will produce good fruit.
Likewise, out of the evil hidden in their hearts,
evil ones will produce what is evil."

Luke 6:45 TPT

The moment we stop feeling the weight of sin, we've already begun to pay the price. The moment we lose that sensitivity toward the Lord is when sin begins to overtake us. But in time, we're each going to become known by the fruit of our lives. When we are under pressure, when we face trials, what's inside is going to come out. We're either going to leak grossness or produce the fruit of God. If we're barren and hardened inside, nothing good is going to come out of our lives. The anointing of Christ, the fullness of joy in a resurrected life, offers to fill us with God's peace. But to experience this filling, we need to stay sensitive to the Spirit. It will show up in our countenance, in our families, in our work, and in so many other areas. Perhaps we may be able to mask our hardness for a while, but pressure proves what we're growing inside, so let's stay close to God, keep our hearts soft, and bring forth goodness in our lives.

ENGAGING HEAVEN

Have you undergone intense pressure lately?
What leaked out?

Roots

"Blessed is the man who trusts in the LORD,
And whose hope is the LORD.
For he shall be like a tree planted by the waters,
Which spreads out its roots by the river."
JEREMIAH 17:7–8 NKJV

God wants us to be stable and strong so we can be effective. God wants us to grow roots like a tree, which is how stability is established. Roots determine our strength, including the depth of our marriages and relationships. How many people do we have in life with whom we can be completely honest? Do we have meaningful and honest accountability? How deep do our roots go in our personal disciplines, convictions, and values? For instance, what dictates our financial decisions, how we spend our time, and where we put our energy? Nobody likes instability. God wants to develop in each of us a root system so we will not be easily blown over in strong winds or storms.

ENGAGING HEAVEN

What sort of personal disciplines can help your roots grow stronger and deeper?

Choosing Wisely

Where there is no counsel, the people fall;
But in the multitude of counselors there is safety.
PROVERBS 11:14 NKJV

Yes, restoration is possible. Of course God loves you. Sure, he has mercy and grace on you. However, good choices starting early are a lot better than good choices starting later. You can have a whole lifetime of bad choices, and God will still redeem and restore you, but there will still be consequences in life for the decisions you made. You might not recover as much as you would have if you'd lived right. So, how can we make wise decisions? People tend to rush into decisions—like a job or a move—before taking time to pray about it and seek wise counsel. Are your intentions biblically based? Have you sought the opinions of people who have lived a little more life than you? They may have a more well-rounded perspective that you haven't obtained yet. Proverbs 18:1 warns us that "a man who isolates himself seeks his own desire; He rages against all wise judgment." We can't be so independent that we neglect to seek counsel.

ENGAGING HEAVEN

Who do you have in your life who can offer you good, godly counsel?

July

Lifestyle of Peace

"Be strong and of good courage;
do not be afraid, nor be dismayed,
for the LORD your God is with you wherever you go."
JOSHUA 1:9 NKJV

Peace is essential. Anxiety is the absence of peace. When we feel hopeless and depressed, it's because peace has left. Whether it's anger, depression, anxiety, or suicidal thoughts, they all manifest in terrible ways. But the truth is, at the heart of the matter, it is a lack of peace. See, one of the challenges of dealing with emotional issues is that the answer the world offers only addresses the symptoms and doesn't solve the underlying cause. It only enables us to cope, not to heal. On the other hand, Jesus has everlasting peace available. When God is not with us, it leaves us feeling hopeless and overwhelmed by the issues of the world, but God wants to restore peace in our hearts. He doesn't want us to feel anxious or filled with fear because he's in power and has everything under control. He wants to teach us to trust him even beyond our limited level of understanding and wants to give us a lifestyle of peace.

ENGAGING HEAVEN

Peace is more powerful than any of the world's problems. Do you feel God's peace even when what is happening around you seems like chaos?

Apart from Me

"Consecrate yourselves therefore,
and be holy, for I am the LORD your God."
LEVITICUS 20:7 NKJV

There's a battle. There's a battle over our children. There's a battle over your soul. There's a battle over this nation. Do you see the spiritual war waging? The church needs to wake up and recognize it. Believers need to wake up to the reality of what is going on around us. We've come as far as we can in our current level of surrender, and it's about time we say no to certain things in our lives. We need to set boundaries for ourselves and go after the better things of God. After all, we can't be filled with anything other than what we're filling ourselves with, what we're receptive to, and what we chase. How can God be in you when you haven't made room for him? It's time to clean house. It's time to set parameters in our lives and make our hearts ready to receive everything the Father has to offer.

ENGAGING HEAVEN

Is there anything in your life you need to consecrate to the Lord?

Faith over Fear

Listen to my testimony:
I cried to God in my distress and he answered me.
He freed me from all my fears!

PSALM 34:4 TPT

God told the Israelites to go and take possession of the land
he had promised them: the land of Canaan. So, in Numbers
13, twelve spies were sent to scout out the land. The report
they brought back was mixed. Ten of them declared that the
inhabitants were too strong and scary and that the Israelites
didn't stand a chance against them. But the other two had a
faith that was bigger than their fear. Their official report was
that the giants were no match for God. There's never going
to be a day in your life when fear will not try to speak. Our
job is to feed our faith so we can dominate that voice, and it
will grow smaller and smaller. But, for all of us, there will still
be moments in life when fear hits us where it hurts, and it is
a challenge to overcome. God has promises for us, but we're
often met with obstacles. We need to recognize that even
if we're no match for those obstacles, they are no match for
God, and he's standing on *our* side.

ENGAGING HEAVEN

It's not that fear isn't real; it's that God is more real.

Pitfalls of Pride

"Yet who knows whether you have come
to the kingdom for such a time as this?"
ESTHER 4:14 NKJV

Haman was an evil man, and he wanted everyone to worship him when he passed by. Everyone consented and bowed except for one Jew named Mordecai. Haman became enraged (3:5). He forgot the millions who bowed down and became fixated on killing not just Mordecai but also the entire Jewish population. This eventually led to his downfall and execution. If Haman had been able to let go of this one thing, he may have gotten away with his evil ways for much longer, but his pride wouldn't allow him. Similarly, King Nebuchadnezzar commanded millions of people to bow to a statue of him, but three friends wouldn't (Daniel 3:12). Do you think he gave his attention to the millions or the three? The three, of course. He threw them into a fire, and Nebuchadnezzar did not come out on top in that story. These two examples show us clearly the potential pitfalls of pride and how detrimental it is to focus on the one or three things going wrong in our life instead of the millions of things going right.

ENGAGING HEAVEN

When the three friends were thrown into the fire, Jesus showed up. Sometimes the clearest way to see Jesus is when you go through fire.

Joy in the Morning

Weeping may endure for a night,
But joy comes in the morning.

PSALM 30:5 NKJV

God doesn't give us everything up front because he knows we couldn't handle it. But God knows everything we're going to face in life, and he has our protection and deliverance prepared for us. He still has a gift of joy that he renews and refreshes every single morning. Let's not lose our sweetness and our joy in life. This life will try to steal it away, but when we remember that we serve a God of joy and that each day is a new day, we can receive that constant refreshing of our joy and rebuilding of our faith. Every time we see a sunrise, we can remember that God's mercy and grace also shine on us each day. And every time we gaze at a sunset, we can realize that the window of life will one day close for each of us and that what we do with our time matters. Life is a series of sunrises and sunsets, and Jesus is our sun. Let's look to him for fresh joy every single morning.

ENGAGING HEAVEN

When was the last time you shared a sunrise alone with Jesus?

A Martyr's Message

"I will not make mention of Him,
Nor speak anymore in His name."
But His word was in my heart like a burning fire
Shut up in my bones.

JEREMIAH 20:9 NKJV

The reason we don't see many martyrs in Western culture today is because we don't preach a message worth dying for. What is the message in your life that's worth dying for? God has given us the Bible; sixty-six books in the original canon that blood was shed over so we could have the message of truth accessible to us today. And through the Word of God and the quickening of the Holy Spirit, we receive a timeless message that doesn't change. Despite what's popular in the world, truth is truth. And with that conviction comes boldness. It's about time the church rises up and draws a line in the sand, making the decision that we're not going to be silenced any longer. We are not going to live trying to blend, and we're not going to live imprisoned to other people's opinions. We're going to stand for truth and live a message that matters.

ENGAGING HEAVEN

What is the message of your life? Are you living for something worth dying for?

God Doesn't Change

The counsel of the LORD stands forever,
The plans of His heart to all generations.

PSALM 33:11 NKJV

Paul warned the church in Ephesus that, although they were doing many great things, they had forgotten their first love, Jesus (Revelation 2:4). When we're not standing steadfast in Christ, when we forget the most fundamental truths, the first thing to get attacked will be our walk with God. The gospel is simple: Christ died on the cross and he paid for us to live and live abundantly. There is no reason for us to be living beneath our privileges. If we are, it's because we chose to. His love doesn't change. His mercy doesn't change. His power doesn't change. We change. The perfect love of the Father makes everything we need accessible to us. The Bible says perfect love casts fear out of our lives (1 John 4:18). Do you live in fear? Fear will infect love like a disease; you can't keep both. Peace is a wonderful gift in God's economy. Do you feel at peace in your life? If you've lost your way, go back to where you stopped experiencing Christ's presence. Go back to your first love.

ENGAGING HEAVEN

Are you still pursuing Jesus with your whole heart and living in his abundance? If not, what changed?

The Kingdom

"But seek first the kingdom of God and His righteousness, and all these things shall be added to you."

MATTHEW 6:33 NKJV

It's not hard to "seek first the kingdom" when you have nothing to lose, but can you "seek first the kingdom" when you have a house, a husband, a family, money, a promotion, a dog, or a cat on the line? Are you just as hungry when you're well fed? It's easy to recognize your need for God when he's your last resort, but is he also your first resort when everything's going perfectly? To seek him when you have options is where the real blessings are found. The beautiful thing is that when it comes to the things of God, you're only ever one step away. There's always hope for full restoration because God is willing to make all things new. There are seasons in your life when you need to seek the kingdom through tears, by pressing in, by calling out. There are other seasons when you can fall back and rest because God is just giving it to you, and all you need to do is receive it like a child. But regardless of what season you are in, your call remains the same: "Seek first the kingdom of God."

ENGAGING HEAVEN

How are you seeking God in the season you are in?

Breaking the Agreement

So above all, guard the affections of your heart,
for they affect all that you are.
Pay attention to the welfare of your innermost being,
for from there flows the wellspring of life.

PROVERBS 4:23 TPT

We are to walk by faith and not by sight, feeling, or fear.
Satan wants you to walk by fear. He has an agreement with
you to be afraid instead of to trust God. But this agreement
will stop you from becoming what God has called you to
be, which means you won't fulfill your purpose in this life.
Fear is the tool that the devil uses to make us miserable, to
destroy our lives. When you live by faith, fear can't rule your
life. You will live peacefully, joyfully, and more abundantly
as you overcome life in Christ. So many times, fear creeps
in with a simple thought. Proverbs 23:7 says, "As he thinks
within himself, so is he" (TPT). See, where the mind goes, the
person follows. Whatever you think, you become. The Bible
makes it very clear that the things you dwell on will dominate
you. Meditate on God's Word and have your mind renewed.
That may sound easy, but it isn't. It means breaking off that
comfortable agreement with fear.

ENGAGING HEAVEN

*Do you have a verse hidden in your heart that you can
meditate on when you feel afraid?*

Highly Offended

The discretion of a man makes him slow to anger,
And his glory is to overlook a transgression.
PROVERBS 19:11 NKJV

How often are you overlooking transgressions? Do you ever? If somebody hurts and offends you, do you let it sink in your heart? The Bible says, "Anger rests in the bosom of fools" (Ecclesiastes 7:9 NKJV). Nothing good comes from being offended; anger can actually make you physically sick! Nothing's going to change in society unless you are the change. Offense is at an all-time high in our culture, and it's up to us to be the change. When someone offends you, are you going to fight back, or are you going to show love? Since when do we change our values based on a subculture? The bait to be offended has already been lured in front of your mouth. Be careful! Because the minute you bite that hook, it's very difficult to get free.

ENGAGING HEAVEN

What steps can you take to remember your values when someone offends you?

Make Preparations

She sets her heart upon a field and takes it as her own.
She labors there to plant the living vines.
She wraps herself in strength, might, and power in all her
works.

PROVERBS 31:16–17 TPT

We're going to make time for what we value, and if we value
our relationship with God, then we'll take fifteen minutes out
of our day to spend with him. How is it that with twenty-
four hours in a day, people think they can't spare fifteen
minutes for their Creator? We spend a lot of time preparing;
we prepare food, homework, assignments for our jobs, and
plans for holiday parties, and we even prepare for accidents.
But it's time we start preparing for eternal things that really
matter. We live in a society motivated by fear and obsessed
with self-preservation; we are always preparing for the
worst when we should be motivated by love. Fulfilling our
calling should be our motivation, remembering that our life
is a vapor anyway (James 4:14). We ought to be spending
some time each day preparing our hearts by spending time
with our Creator. He is who will lead us and preserve us and
prepare us for anything that's to come.

ENGAGING HEAVEN

What motivates you?

Forgive and Move On

Do not hasten in your spirit to be angry,
For anger rests in the bosom of fools.

<small>ECCLESIASTES 7:9 NKJV</small>

How do you deal with people hurting you? How do you handle your heart when somebody violates you or breaks your trust? One of the most integral parts to having a close relationship with God is forgiveness. We absolutely *have* to guard our hearts against becoming bitter by holding on to the injustices people have inflicted on us. Even if the other person never asks for forgiveness or even shows no remorse, it's essential that we find a way to forgive him or her truly from our hearts because, ultimately, it has everything to do with us and our ability to move on in a healthy way. Unforgiveness is like a match in a wastebasket full of paper. Undealt with, the whole house will eventually burn up. Face it, forgive, and move on. Because Christ forgave us, we are able to forgive others. In fact, because Christ forgave us, we are *expected* to forgive others.

ENGAGING HEAVEN

What is holding you back from escaping the prison of unforgiveness?

Positivity

I will worship you, Yahweh, with extended hands
as my whole heart erupts with praise!
I will tell everyone everywhere about your wonderful works!
PSALM 9:1 TPT

Is there anything more disheartening than a Christian who is not positive? Negativity breeds discontent and doubt, and we need to train our spirits to think and respond differently. I'm not saying we ought to ignore issues but rather that positivity matters in every situation. Let's tap into that eternal optimism. No matter what you're going through, no matter what situation you're in, thank God. In the midst of the darkest days, we still have the Lord on our side, and that's enough. There is always a reason to have faith and hope and thanksgiving. The Bible says to think about things that are true, noble, just, pure, lovely, of good report, virtuous, and praiseworthy (Philippians 4:8). So, when you feel frustrated and your body is exhausted or you're emotionally fried and the kids are driving you crazy, stop and give thanks. That's how you live positively.

ENGAGING HEAVEN

What areas in life are the quickest to set you off? Spend some time praying specifically about these situations before you encounter them.

Dead Bones

"I will put My Spirit in you, and you shall live,
and I will place you in your own land.
Then you shall know that I, the Lord,
have spoken it and performed it."

Ezekiel 37:14 NKJV

The Bible promises that when we hunger and thirst for
righteousness, we will be filled (Matthew 5:6). The truth
is that we can have as much of God as we want. If we're
satisfied with a little, then that's all we're going to get. But if
we're hungry for more, then he's going to meet that desire
and fill us with more and more of him. In Ezekiel 37, God
showed the prophet a valley of dry bones and told him to
speak to them, to prophesy over them that they would live.
Ezekiel did, and the bones came back to life! God can take
dead things and bring them back to life, but it takes an act of
faith. When we declare our desperation for him, our insatiable
hunger for him, he will fill us and use us and bring our dead
bones back to life.

ENGAGING HEAVEN

*Are you satisfied with where you are with God, or are you
hungry for more?*

Nudge from the Nest

"As an eagle stirs up its nest,
Hovers over its young,
Spreading out its wings, taking them up,
Carrying them on its wings..."
DEUTERONOMY 32:11 NKJV

The reason a mother eagle stirs her nest is because she wants the baby to get out and fly. And before long, that eaglet will find herself in a compromising position because her mother will actually nudge her out of the nest. With no idea how to fly, the eaglet will fall at a frightening pace until suddenly her mom swoops down and catches her, taking her back to the nest where the process repeats until the eaglet finally understands she has no choice but to fly. We were created to fly, but how likely is it that we will ever break out of our comfort zones without a nudge? Perhaps it's *not* the devil making us feel uncomfortable after all; perhaps it's the nudge of our loving Father who wants us to live our best lives and learn to fly. We don't like feeling vulnerable or out of control, but sometimes that's the only way our faith will grow and we will learn to soar. And, no matter what, God is going to be there to catch us when we fall.

ENGAGING HEAVEN

Do you feel uncomfortable or out of control?
Why do you think that might be?

Bound by Principles

"Martha, Martha, you are worried
and troubled about many things.
But one thing is needed,
and Mary has chosen that good part,
which will not be taken away from her."

Luke 10:41–42 NKJV

There are so many people who don't understand the presence of God. They dive further and further into upholding principles because that's what is easiest for their flesh. But a life with God wasn't made to be lived bound by principles only. Principles come out of value systems and relationship. Principles devoid of relationship and love are death. How is it that somebody can read the Bible and adhere to biblical values and yet be as angry as a hornet, be as demonic as the devil? What happened? Where's the disconnect? The disconnect is that there is no life-giving love that comes from relationship. See, we want a set of rules to live by because that's the easiest way to check our Christian boxes and feel like we're living right, but God's desire is for a relationship. When you let go of all the struggles, the pain, and the frustration and you just love God, the Word of God comes alive in your heart and fills you with the revelation and wisdom you need to uphold God's principles. It can't happen the other way around.

ENGAGING HEAVEN

Are you worried and troubled about many things?
Lay them at the foot of the cross today.

Inspiration

Wisdom opens your heart to receive wise counsel,
but pride closes your ears to advice
and gives birth only to quarrels and strife.
PROVERBS 13:10 TPT

There is a place of wisdom. The Bible says it's found in a multitude of counselors (Proverbs 11:14). Having healthy people in your life to draw inspiration from is an important step to becoming wise. Find people who are healthier, stronger, and more spiritually mature than you. Draw inspiration from them, learn from them, and ask their advice. They can help lead you in the right direction. Don't discount the value of having godly mother and father figures in your life. If you don't have a desire to seek out godly counsel, you're not going to find wisdom. None of us is a lone ranger; God created us for community and accountability. And when it comes to walking in wisdom, those with whom you surround yourself will play an important part in that journey.

ENGAGING HEAVEN

Consider the people God has placed in your life.
Are you seeking out wisdom?

Light of the World

"You are the light of the world.
A city that is set on a hill cannot be hidden."
MATTHEW 5:14 NKJV

Jesus did not say you are the light of your street. He didn't say you are the light of your job or a lamp on a nightstand in the corner. He put a light in you and said you are the light of the *world*. As the light of the world, we don't need to become so caught up in political elections or incomes or prestige that we cease shining the light of Christ. The light of the world recognizes that God has given us his Holy Spirit, and we have been given power to accomplish his purposes. There is not a darkness on this earth that the light inside us cannot break through. All we need is for believers to believe. Jesus did not just die on the cross so we could escape earth and go to heaven. He came so that we may have abundant life now on earth (John 10:10). Say yes to God and realize that nothing can stand against us when we carry the light of Christ. God has equipped us, filled us, and sent us.

ENGAGING HEAVEN

What does it look like in your life to be the light of the world? In your household? In your workplace? In relationships?

Believe

For he came as a witness,
to point the way to the Light of Life,
and to help everyone believe.

JOHN 1:7 TPT

All the way through the book of John we read numerous accounts that tell us to believe. In fact, John the apostle used the life of John the Baptist as an example of faith because the entire goal of the Baptist's life *was* to bear witness so that we could believe. The words *believe* and *believer* show up in the book of John sixty-three times. When you are a daughter of God, you bear his attributes. You start thinking like Jesus, you start acting like Jesus, you start responding like Jesus, praying for the sick like Jesus, believing for miracles like Jesus, and seeing increase like Jesus. Why? Because as God's daughter, following his example, believing in his Word, you pick up all the characteristics of your Father. It's important to understand that belief and trust are the only things that will get you there. So, as a daughter of the King, have faith in your Father.

ENGAGING HEAVEN

Are you the kind of witness whose life encourages others to believe?

Expecting Too Much

"When you follow me as my disciple,
you must put aside
your father, your mother, your wife,
your sisters, your brothers;
it will even seem as though you hate your own life."
Luke 14:26 TPT

People are not perfect. Every relationship will ultimately
let you down eventually. A lot of times we put in people an
exuberant amount of trust that should only be placed in
God. If we're expecting something from another person that
only God is fit to give, we're going to be disappointed, and
our relationship will be in trouble. This is especially true with
marriages because of the close intimacy we have with that
our spouses. Ladies, if you get married hoping for all your
emptiness to be filled and dreams to be satisfied, you're in for
a rude awakening. It's not going to happen because only God
can offer that level of fulfillment. Only God will never break
his promises. Only God will never hurt you. He is the friend
who sticks closer than a brother (Proverbs 18:24). He's the
father to the fatherless and the defender of widows (Psalm
68:5). We can give ourselves completely to God, and then we
begin to trust God in others.

ENGAGING HEAVEN

*Are you using other people to fill a void in your life that only
God can fill?*

Invitations

He said to the disciples,
"It is impossible that no offenses should come,
but woe to him through whom they do come!"
LUKE 17:1 NKJV

Jesus said offenses are going to come. Nobody on the planet is exempt from being offended; we've all received several sparkling invitations to become offended. The question is, what do we do with offense? The Bible warns us to guard our hearts diligently because all the issues of life flow out of it (Proverbs 4:23). If your heart is hurt and offended and you're living with bitterness and frustration inside you, it will eventually end up being the death of you spiritually. The Bible says anger is hidden in the belly of a fool (Ecclesiastes 7:9). Once we invite offense in, it's very difficult to get it back out. Why live in torment for years? Why give your offender that much power over your mind? Why give the devil a foothold? When offense hands you an invitation, rip that thing up. Don't attend that party.

ENGAGING HEAVEN

Who has offended you recently? What can you do about it?

Aim High

"He who is faithful in what is least is faithful also in much;
and he who is unjust in what is least is unjust also in much."
Luke 16:10 NKJV

Aim high. Do you realize that you're giving yourself and your
life to the things you're believing for? What does that look
like for you? What does success look like? What does your
life look like if your family is healthy and you're walking in the
power of God? What does it look like when you give yourself
to a spiritual purpose? You are on this earth to see the gospel
of the Lord Jesus Christ transform lives. That sounds great in
theory, but what does it look like? Don't let the lack of vision
in those around you deter you. Don't let doubters talk you
out of it. Believe God, aim high, write your vision down, and
make it clear. What has God given you, and what are you
doing with it? What vision has he laid on your heart. Do you
believe it is possible to accomplish it?

ENGAGING HEAVEN

*Write down your vision and whatever things in your life you
are believing God for.*

Your Hair Matters

"The very hairs of your head are all numbered.
Do not fear therefore;
you are of more value than many sparrows."
Luke 12:7 NKJV

God cares about the little things. He cares about every detail of your life because he cares about you. And how we see God will determine who we believe he is. If we understand that he is loving, faithful, true, and trustworthy, then we will be much more apt to receive from him. We limit what we receive from God because we don't understand his nature. Do you realize that God knows the number of hairs that are on your head? Even your hair matters to God! If you can have faith for salvation and for the miraculous, then you can have faith for your pet, your job, your expenses. Faith is faith. If God cares about birds and grass, how much more do you believe he cares about you (Matthew 6:26–30)? Whatever is on your mind today, you can talk to God freely about it because he cares too.

ENGAGING HEAVEN

What is it that matters to you and that you are struggling to believe also matters to God?

Integrity Matters

"Whatever you have spoken in private will be public knowledge, and what you have whispered secretly behind closed doors will be broadcast far and wide for all to hear."
Luke 12:3 TPT

Integrity is revealed in who you are when nobody else is around. There's a quote by Joe Frazier that says, "Champions aren't made in the ring; they are merely recognized there." That means long before someone becomes a boxing champion, they endure a lot of hard work, training, and dedication. We get to see them when they're crowned, but their character and worth were established long before then behind the scenes. And that's the truth in our spiritual lives as well. Those battles behind the scenes are what prepare us for greatness. They are what reveals who we are when nobody is looking. They are the multitude of little things that prepare us for the big reveals God has coming. If we don't pass the behind-the-scenes tests, we're not going to be ready for the ring. We will never see it revealed in front of people. Character is essential for the Christian life. Strive to be the same person behind closed doors as you are in front of others.

ENGAGING HEAVEN

How has your integrity been tested lately?

Building Your Legacy

I thank God, whom I serve
with a pure conscience, as my forefathers did.
2 TIMOTHY 1:3 NKJV

Paul included in his letter to Timothy, "I call to remembrance the genuine faith that is in you, which dwelt first in your grandmother Lois and your mother Eunice, and I am persuaded is in you also" (2 Timothy 1:5 NKJV). We are each leaving behind a legacy. What kind of legacy are you leaving? A legacy or heritage is normally thought of as the amount of money or material worth you leave behind, but that's only a very small part of it. The greatest thing you can leave behind for your kids or your loved ones is your spiritual legacy. Leave behind a heritage of loving God and knowing God. You're the daughter of God. And whether you realize it or not, whether you have kids or not, you're building a spiritual legacy. When you die, nobody is going to wonder how much your 401(k) was. Did you live a life that mattered? Are people going to remember you for the things you can't see?

ENGAGING HEAVEN

What legacy is your life writing?

Attention

But we all, with unveiled face,
beholding as in a mirror the glory of the Lord,
are being transformed into the same image
from glory to glory, just as by the Spirit of the Lord.
2 Corinthians 3:18 NKJV

The currency of our generation seems to be attention. We really crave attention. People go to great lengths to get noticed. They leave churches because they're not noticed. They equate attention with validation. But our self-worth isn't found in Instagram likes or the number of friends who follow us on Facebook. Fame and attention are not what is most important; they are not the keys to a good life. What happens when people look at you? Everything you are gets revealed and magnified. Fame, attention, and worldly success expose a person very quickly. Would you be proud of what people see? There's a tranquility and a peace found through having a life hidden in Jesus. When it's his attention that we seek, he gives it, and we become more like *him*. It's not about getting views and likes and applause. It's about living a life that counts and makes a difference for the gospel.

ENGAGING HEAVEN

Whose attention do you seek? That of the empty, fickle world? Or the one who holds everything?

Burn the Record

Love does not traffic in shame and disrespect,
nor selfishly seek its own honor.
Love is not easily irritated or quick to take offense.

1 CORINTHIANS 13:5 TPT

When someone wrongs you, do you act like Christ and forgive them, or do you keep a detailed file of their wrongdoings on hand for later, pulling out papers and saving them as damning evidence every time a new argument arises? Love plays an important part—in fact, the lead role—because the Bible points out that love does not keep a record of wrongs. Love doesn't compile a case. Love deals with each situation anew and doesn't dig up the past. The past has been forgiven. Love is God's system, which is always characterized by grace. There's no debt to be paid because the one who loves is willing to forgive the offense and to burn the record. After all, how can we not forgive when Christ forgave us? How can we not extend love to others when he extended his love to us?

ENGAGING HEAVEN

Is there a record book you need to burn?

Rejoicing and Weeping

Rejoice with those who rejoice,
and weep with those who weep.
ROMANS 12:15 NKJV

Everyone is walking through a different season. You may be in a valley right now, or you may be on a mountaintop. Regardless of where on the path you are, it's important to remember that Jesus never changes. He is there with us in the good and the bad. Our ugly days do not scare him off. If we're going to "rejoice with those who rejoice" and "weep with those who weep," we need to learn how to love like Jesus. Often, these two sentiments will happen at the same time with different friends. Are we intimidated to sit in their sorrow with them? Can we rejoice with our friends when our own journey is winding through the valley? God has called each of us down a different path, but what isn't different is his willingness to take every step alongside us. So, as children of God, let's walk the same way and be there for our loved ones in the good and the bad.

ENGAGING HEAVEN

Be confident in who God has called you to be because there are no accidents in his kingdom. You are in the palm of his hand, in the fabric of what he is creating on this earth, and you are blessed in every way.

Heartbreak Hill

For that reason, I don't run just for exercise
or box like one throwing aimless punches,
but I train like a champion athlete.
I subdue my body and get it under my control,
so that after preaching the good news to others
I myself won't be disqualified.

1 CORINTHIANS 9:26-27 TPT

Paul was explaining to the Greeks, "Look, you take care of
your body. You don't eat bad food, and you keep yourselves in
great physical shape, but we're running a heavenly race, and
it is far more important. That takes even more discipline than
our physical bodies!" Many people start out excited on this
race of Christianity, but the minute we face heartbreak hill, we
get disqualified. Christianity is filled with heartbreak hills, but
that's not where the race ends. Regardless of what obstacle
is standing in the way, we have an assured victory if only we
persevere. And so today, wherever you are, wherever you're
running, understand that God has designed this spiritual race
and that we fight with purpose. We race to receive a crown
that will never perish. Maybe you're running downhill right
now, and it feels good. Well, keep the pace and get ready
because another incline is coming. We are not shocked or
dismayed because our hope and our trust is in God.

ENGAGING HEAVEN

*What spiritual disciplines and training do you practice so
that you're prepared for the tough times when they come?*

Low Living

When Jesus saw him lying there,
he knew that the man had been crippled for a long time.
Jesus said to him, "Do you truly long to be well?"
JOHN 5:6 TPT

Faith is designed to raise your expectations. See, a lot of people don't step out because of fear of disappointment. They live low. When every day looks the same in your life, that is an indication that your light is going out. You have started giving up, or your faith has plateaued. If you are the smartest person in the room, run! Surround yourself with people who are doing better, reaching farther, and inspiring you toward greater things. Jesus asked a man who had been paralyzed for thirty-eight years if he wanted to get better. When you see better, you do better, and that's how you'll get better. Don't let your light go out and don't make excuses for low expectations. God wants to raise your expectations and empower you to do great things for him. Believe in greater things ahead.

ENGAGING HEAVEN

Besides this one, what book are you reading now? Reading is inspirational, and readers tend to be more successful. Is what you're reading helping you remain motivated?

Balanced Christian Diet

From that time on many of the disciples
turned their backs on Jesus
and refused to be associated with him.
JOHN 6:66 TPT

There's a danger in not having a balanced Christian diet. When you have a limited diet, you become vulnerable. For instance, everyone wants to eat bread, but when Jesus said, "Unless you eat the flesh of the Son of Man and drink His blood, you have no life in you" (John 6:53 NKJV), most people, including many of his disciples, left and walked with him no more. Ladies, we cannot live wrong and die right. We cannot walk away from the things of God, no matter how distasteful they may seem. He said we need to take his cup, eat his flesh, and drink his blood. Unless we're going to eat with him when it's delicious as well as when it's disgusting, we're going to starve to death. Jesus offers salvation and forgiveness, but he also offers sanctification.

ENGAGING HEAVEN

What Bible verses or commands do you find distasteful or difficult? Pray today for God to reveal to you his love and reasoning through them.

August

Faith Rest Life

To be carnally minded is death,
but to be spiritually minded is life and peace.
ROMANS 8:6 NKJV

Striving is a pit. So many people spend their lives striving!
They fight with their spouse, they're frustrated at their kids,
they're upset their house is a mess, and they stress about
finances. Just breathe. Responsibilities matter but stop
letting carnal things control you. The carnal mind is the
enemy of God; it's at war with him, and it's his opposite.
We're called to live according to the Spirit. Why? Because
that leads to life. Focusing only on carnal things is literally
leading us to our death: to a dead, purposeless existence.
Stop striving and start abiding. Busyness is a trap. We
cannot start our days out anxious, frustrated, and stressed
and expect to walk out in the Spirit. A striving mind, a mind
fixated on the flesh, cannot connect with God. Take a few
minutes in the morning to just worship, pray, and spiritually
prepare for the day because the voice of God is going to be
heard in a whisper. He is found in rest.

ENGAGING HEAVEN

*This week, shut everything out. Let the busyness go.
Let the confusion go and just be with God.*

No Substitute

"The Helper, the Holy Spirit,
whom the Father will send in My name,
He will teach you all things,
and bring to your remembrance all things that I said to you."
JOHN 14:26 NKJV

As great as therapists, pastors, parents, and friends are, there are some things that we just can't get unless we listen to the Lord and make time for the Father. People today are hurting themselves by spending so much time on the internet and by not having real meaningful relationships, the most important being the one we have with God. Truthfully, we were made for community and for relationships. Out of loneliness, we all need somebody to talk to and to help us process our thoughts and decisions. But we can't replace the work of the Holy Spirit with any person and try to excuse our relationship with God in this process. Yes, invest in other people and establish meaningful relationships. Yes, heed wise counsel and get help from whomever you need it. But first and foremost, seek the Lord, listen to him, and make that the highest priority relationship you have.

ENGAGING HEAVEN

There is never going to be a substitute for a surrendered life. There's never going to be a substitute for getting on our faces and just listening to the Father and spending alone time with him. Do that today.

Go after Peace

"Peace I leave with you, My peace I give to you;
not as the world gives do I give to you.
Let not your heart be troubled, neither let it be afraid."

JOHN 14:27 NKJV

Peace is essential. It's our birthright. We shouldn't make a move without it, and yet people make decisions all the time without first making sure their "peace maker" is intact. If it's broken or if you're under physical or emotional attack, that is not a good time to make decisions. Temptation to make brazen decisions before we've found peace about them will result in paying a price, and it often involves backtracking. It's essential that we make up our minds to go after peace. Peace is our anchor, our guide, and our decision maker. It's our gut check. To find peace, we have to slow our pace and listen. Try meditating on a Bible verse, praying, or listening to a worship song. Start each day by focusing your heart and your mind on God instead of getting immediately caught up in the concerns of the world. When you spend time with God, specifically ask for peace. When you face difficult situations, seek peace *before* making any decisions.

ENGAGING HEAVEN

Do you long for breakthrough in your life, but no matter how hard you try you feel like it's not coming? Start each day by pursuing peace. The rest will follow.

Pharisee Faith

Pursue love, and desire spiritual gifts,
but especially that you may prophesy.
1 CORINTHIANS 14:1 NKJV

Do you desire spiritual gifts? We must thirst for the things of
God, and that includes spiritual gifts. It requires faithfulness.
It requires pursuing God. It requires going further than our
comfort zones to truthfully desire his gifts. We have to learn
to go that extra mile, to be diligent, to give extra. Do you
believe in miracles and truly expect to see the power of God?
If we want to see him at work, let's engage in his work. Let's
worship, pray, feed the poor, and love our neighbors even
when it's hard. Let's serve our families. Christianity was never
meant to be a one-time prayer to safeguard against hell.
To be a Christian means to be an active part of what Christ
is doing. It means we follow in the footsteps of Christ. The
gospel doesn't stop at salvation; he paid for much, much
more than that on the cross, and he wants to open our eyes
to greater things than we can possibly imagine.

ENGAGING HEAVEN

*Have you prayed for spiritual gifts? Are you prepared to use
what he blesses you with for his glory?*

Abide

"I am the vine, you are the branches.
He who abides in Me, and I in him, bears much fruit;
for without Me you can do nothing."
JOHN 15:5 NKJV

"Bearing much fruit" comes from abiding. That's the opposite mentality the world adheres to. We're told to hustle and make it happen. We're pressured to believe that success only comes through countless nights of chasing "the dream." But we're trying too hard. Before you head out into the rat race of life, spend time with the Lord and get in his Word. Get your heart focused and your priorities straightened out. There is no question we live in the most distracted times, which is why it's more important than ever to sit at his feet *first*. It's about abiding, not about striving. In Luke 10, Mary chose "the better thing" by temporarily setting aside household demands to spend time with Jesus first. That can be hard to do, but our priority always has to be our relationship with him. It won't take long to realize that all our other fruit grows more abundantly when we do.

ENGAGING HEAVEN

Read Luke 10:38–42. Do you relate more to Mary or Martha?

Fragrance

We have become the unmistakable aroma of the victory
of the Anointed One to God—a perfume of life to those being
saved and the odor of death to those who are perishing.

2 Corinthians 2:15 TPT

Besides being incredibly strong, the cedar tree was at one
point the most exported tree in the world because it was
rot-free, bug-free, and had a fragrance that confounded
everybody. The fragrance that exudes from the cedar tree
made it one of the most appealing trees on the planet, and
this is the tree God compares us to in the Bible (Psalm 92:12).
Christians will be known by their fragrance. Perhaps you
started out your Christian journey sweet and fragrant; you lit
up the room when you walked in, and everyone was drawn to
your smile. Do you still smile? Are you still permeating Jesus
and sweetness on everyone around you? Life can cause rot
and send bugs to break us down, so it's important that we
keep growing in Christ, dispel the rot, and never lose our
fragrance.

ENGAGING HEAVEN

*Can you think of someone who carries a sweet "fragrance"
with them wherever they go? Why do you think that is? Do
you carry such a fragrance?*

Promotion through Pain

Do you not know that those who run in a race all run,
but one receives the prize?
Run in such a way that you may obtain it.
1 CORINTHIANS 9:24 NKJV

It's easy to start strong, but can you finish strong? We need to pray in order to be filled with the power to finish. In life, it's the tests that bring promotion. A student passes a final exam to continue on to the next grade. An applicant passes an interview to land the job and then is judged by her efforts to be eligible for a promotion. An athlete is recruited based on her performance, which is only possible through the pain of endless practice. Well, just as we are tested physically for promotions and advancements in life, we are tested spiritually too. Promotion is hidden in the pain. Testimony is discovered in the test. In Greek culture, they didn't have a second place. Everybody competed for first place. Paul used this understanding to describe how adamantly we should run this spiritual race. The athletes went through rigorous training, all for a crown that was temporary. But as Christians, we run this race for the Lord, for a crown that will last forever.

ENGAGING HEAVEN

Are you running? Are you training?
Do you want the promotion?

Be the Light

Beloved, don't be obsessed with taking revenge,
but leave that to God's righteous justice.
For the Scriptures say: "Vengeance is mine,
and I will repay," says the Lord.

ROMANS 12:19 TPT

Vengeance belongs to the Lord. We have to put justice in
the hands of God. When we experience injustice, it is an
opportunity to be the light of Christ in a world so fixated
on demanding what is fair. Everyone wants what they have
coming to them, but as Christians, we want the Lord. God
will vindicate you on your behalf and in his perfect timing.
If somebody wrongs you and you try to demand justice in
your own strength, you then have to maintain it in your own
strength. If, however, you conceive it in faith, you'll receive
it in faith. That means placing it in God's hands, trusting his
timing, and letting it go.

ENGAGING HEAVEN

*Have you suffered wrongdoing or injustice by the hands
of someone else? How did you react? Were you able to
give it to God, let it go, and find peace and forgiveness
in your heart?*

Mortify the Members

If you live according to the flesh you will die;
but if by the Spirit you put to death the deeds of the body,
you will live.

ROMANS 8:13 NKJV

Colossians 3:5 says, "Put to death your members which are on the earth" (NKJV). What does that mean? It means toxic mindsets that will hurt you such as jealousy, evil thoughts, and offense. That's what it means to mortify the members. Kill the things in your life that are trying to become part of you and take you over. This is a matter of life and death because if you keep satisfying the flesh and ignoring the nudging of the Spirit, your own spirit is going to grow cold and die. It's not possible for two kingdoms to coexist within you; you have to submit to one or the other. The world calls out to you every day, telling you that you need more money or a man or greater prestige. Your spirit and your values are under constant attack. But that is all a lie. Put it to death. God is also calling out to you today, saying he has something better in store for you. He offers *real* wealth, *real* love, and *real* identity.

ENGAGING HEAVEN

Which fleshly, evil members do you need to mortify?
What alternative promises is God offering you?

Changing Roles

"No longer do I call you servants,
for a servant does not know what his master is doing;
but I have called you friends,
for all things that I heard from My Father
I have made known to you."
JOHN 15:15 NKJV

If you think and act like a slave, you probably are one. Are you still a slave to your sins, or are you benefiting from all the Father has for you as his daughter? Slaves are always in competition with one another. If you find yourself constantly striving and comparing yourself with other people, you're probably still thinking like a slave. If you're driven by a search for significance and you fail to understand how significant you are as a child of God, you're probably still thinking like a slave. It's time to change the role, act like a friend, act like a daughter, and break off the mentality of being an orphan and a slave. When you do this and you start living in your birthright, you will see an abundant life ahead of you.

ENGAGING HEAVEN

What are some indicators that you still have an orphan mindset and not a daughter mindset?

How Will They Hear?

How then shall they call on Him
in whom they have not believed?
And how shall they believe in Him
of whom they have not heard?
And how shall they hear without a preacher?

ROMANS 10:14 NKJV

It's God's will that none would perish (2 Peter 3:9), but many do. Why do they perish? Well, one of the reasons is because we're not opening our mouths. If we're not willing to share the gospel of the Lord Jesus Christ, how are they going to know about him? If we're not willing to step out and show Christ's love, how will the gospel spread? Jesus took a huge step by coming from heaven to earth and demonstrating for us what perfect love looks like. Now he has commissioned us to follow his example and love one another. How will others hear if we don't open our hearts, open our mouths, open our homes, and tell them? With all the love we have received, the least we can do is share it with others.

ENGAGING HEAVEN

What are some of the different ways you can both tell and demonstrate the love of Christ to someone who has not accepted him yet?

Resistance

Let this hope burst forth within you,
releasing a continual joy.
Don't give up in a time of trouble,
but commune with God at all times.
ROMANS 12:12 TPT

What is your reaction to facing resistance in life? Do you complain or become disheartened because it's so difficult? Have you ever considered that it might be by design? Resistance actually helps us. If you've ever been to the gym, you realize that it's only through struggling and enduring that you build muscle. It's resistance training. Intense pressure turns coal into diamonds. Even airplanes fly on resistance. In a culture that doesn't want resistance and doesn't want to feel uncomfortable, we learn to associate resistance with problems. But just because life is a little rocky doesn't necessarily mean something is wrong. Sometimes it's by design. Sometimes the Lord allows things into our lives to mold us into something greater. He allows tests and trials for our benefit. But if we're always looking at it as a problem, how will we ever learn the solution? Sometimes difficult things happen to us, and we have to learn to be okay with that.

ENGAGING HEAVEN

What is the solution to resistance?

A Different Form

"My own sheep will hear my voice
and I know each one, and they will follow me."
John 10:27 TPT

Second Kings 6:8–23 tells a powerful story about Elisha
and his servant. The king of Aram sent a mighty army full
of horses and chariots to capture Elisha, and when Elisha's
servant saw them approaching, he panicked. But Elisha
wasn't worried at all. Instead, he prayed that God would open
the eyes of his servant, and he did. The servant looked and
saw the hills surrounding them were covered with the army
of the Lord—horses and chariots of fire. He had been so
scared of the enemy, but Elisha trusted the voice of God. No
matter what you're going through, just learn to recognize the
voice of the Lord. He is going to take care of you. He moves
on your behalf. Faith knows that, even if an army is marching
against you, God will show up in ways you never expect.

ENGAGING HEAVEN

Do you know what the voice of the Lord sounds like?
Are your eyes fixed on him?

Without Distraction

The urgency of our times mean that from now on,
those who have wives should live as though without them.

1 Corinthians 7:29 TPT

The purpose of Paul's words is found in verse 35: "That you may serve the Lord without distraction" (NKJV). If we're married, we're supposed to live as if we were single regarding our devotion to Jesus. We must serve God as if he is our only devotion. Yes, serve your family. Yes, invest in a great marriage. Yes, spend time with your kids. But you're not strong for anybody unless you're strong yourself. It's so important that Jesus remains your priority in order for you to be the best wife, mother, grandmother, sister, daughter, student, employee, friend, or neighbor that you can be. The incredible mystery about focusing your heart on Jesus first is that, as you prioritize your spiritual life with God, all those other worries in life start to fall in line. When trials come, what's inside is going to come out. It's inevitable. God has a plan for you, but you can't operate at full capacity if you're hurting on the inside and not taking time to hear from God daily. That's the power of devotion.

ENGAGING HEAVEN

What are you doing to protect your daily time with God?

Break Free

We know that all things work together for good to those who love God, to those who are the called according to His purpose. For whom He foreknew, He also predestined to be conformed to the image of His Son.

ROMANS 8:28–29 NKJV

When you are born in the Spirit of God, you are born into royalty. You are born into God's best for you. It's time for you to get free. It's time for you to break out of what you have always known. You are no longer defined by your trauma or your mistakes; you are defined as a daughter of the Most High. When Shadrach, Meshach, and Abednego emerged unharmed from the fiery furnace, the Bible says they didn't even have the smell of fire on them or on their clothes (Daniel 3:27). The same is going to be said about you after you emerge victorious from the difficult seasons you walk through: there won't even be a hint of the smell of trauma on you. You are going to run free. People may meet you at the beginning of your book or somewhere in the middle, but nobody knows how your story ends. Only God knows. So, don't worry about what people think about you. It's time to trust God like never before and watch miracles happen in your life.

ENGAGING HEAVEN

Do you define yourself by your mistakes or by who God says you are?

Loving Storms

After many days of seeing neither the sun nor the stars, and with the violent storm continuing to rage against us, all hope of ever getting through it alive was abandoned.

ACTS 27:20 TPT

You're not going to live a life with no friction, no matter how hard you try to create a safe haven and live in a bubble. If there's no wind and no resistance, then there's also no victory. We live in a world that constantly brings resistance and storms and tests, all so we can watch God's strength at work. In any storm, the most important thing is being anchored. Paul and the sailors must have understood this because the Bible says they dropped four anchors (v. 29). The Word of God is our anchor. As long as we're anchored in it, no storm can destroy us. The Word of God is his promise to us, and we can rest assured that things will happen just as he said. In the midst of the storm, Paul reassured his men by saying, "Therefore take heart, men, for I believe God that it will be just as it was told me" (v. 25 NKJV).

ENGAGING HEAVEN

Resistance encourages prayer. What would compel you to pray if everything in your life were perfect?

Celebrate

"Most assuredly, I say to you, he who believes in Me,
the works that I do he will do also;
and greater works than these he will do,
because I go to My Father."

JOHN 14:12 NKJV

Are you hung up on some things you don't understand? Does your heart struggle because you're confused as to why life happened the way it did? Do you demand answers of God? Instead of always asking why, let's start reading the Word of God, praying, and hearing from the Holy Spirit. Instead of living in the realm of regret and posing questions that are rooted in ulterior motives, what if we recognize that everything we need is found in his presence—including peace and understanding? We like to be in control but demanding it of God will only lead us further and further into unbelief and doubt. We are, after all, just passing through on this earth to do the will of the Father. We have plenty of reasons to celebrate. We can celebrate that we get to do the works of God.

ENGAGING HEAVEN

Are there things you need to release control of and get back to trusting God? Are there unanswered questions that you need to free your mind and your heart from by believing God and in his goodness to reign?

Know What You Have

Peter said, "I don't have money, but I'll give you this—
by the power of the name of Jesus Christ of Nazareth,
stand up and walk!"

Acts 3:6 TPT

It's important to have the self-awareness to realize what
we have and what we don't have. We can't give somebody
something we don't have. Peter and John were not wealthy
men, but they knew God had given them healing power. Peter
said, "What I do have I give you" (NKJV). So many believers
today couldn't say that because they don't know what they
have. If you don't know what's yours, how can you declare
it? If you don't fully realize what God has given you, how
can you walk in its power? One of the greatest tragedies of
Christianity today is how so many people pray to God for
things he has already given them. Why are we begging God
to never leave us when he already said he wouldn't? We're
wasting our time if we continue to pray these unscriptural
requests. How can we find the confidence to say, "Rise up and
walk"? By understanding what we have. It's all in the Bible.

ENGAGING HEAVEN

What has God given you, according to the Scriptures?

Attitude of Faith

For I say, through the grace given to me, to everyone who is among you, not to think of himself more highly than he ought to think, but to think soberly, as God has dealt to each one a measure of faith.

ROMANS 12:3 NKJV

Attitude is important. Our faith has an attitude. Faith is so misunderstood. It is not hocus-pocus. It is real, and it is the greatest commodity on the earth. More than silver, more than gold, faith is what will actually get you where you need to go. What's more, faith is something everybody has, but few people have an attitude of faith. What does that mean? Well, the Bible says that God gave a measure of faith to each of us. See, faith isn't something we're trying to find or earn. Faith is a muscle that needs to be exercised. We all have it, but we don't all use it. Faith as small as a mustard seed can move mountains (Matthew 17:20), but how many mountains do we see moving? Whether or not we feel like we have faith...we have it. What we need to do is exercise it by cultivating an attitude of faith.

ENGAGING HEAVEN

How can you exercise your faith this week?

The Road to Repentance

Do you despise the riches of His goodness,
forbearance, and longsuffering,
not knowing that the goodness of God
leads you to repentance?

ROMANS 2:4 NKJV

We will never step into our full identity or purpose if we think God is a mean King who constantly disapproves of us. There's a propagated picture of a cruel God who hates people and wants to send them to hell, but that's not the real God. Condemnation rarely brings about change. Rather, it's his goodness that brings us to repentance and ushers change in. There is definitely a connection between our view of God and our identity. When we understand God's nature and how he operates, we can receive his love and step into our true callings. But how can we receive who God really is if we don't have a good relationship with him? So many people only go running to him when they've sinned or their life is a mess. But if we want fear broken off and our peace restored, guess what? "Perfect love casts out fear" (1 John 4:18 NKJV). God's love is what is going to make the difference.

ENGAGING HEAVEN

How do you see God? What does that say about your relationship with him?

Perfect Patience

That's not all! Even in times of trouble
we have a joyful confidence,
knowing that our pressures will
develop in us patient endurance.
And patient endurance will refine our character,
and proven character leads us back to hope.

ROMANS 5:3–4 TPT

Paul says patience comes first before hope. As we exercise
patient endurance, as we extend grace to others and
ourselves, it refines our characters and fills us with hope.
Additionally, this is the sort of hope that never disappoints
because it's far more than simply wishful thinking. This hope,
gained through patience and the refinement of our character,
is the proper perspective of God's guaranteed promises. We
can be confidently patient because we *know* what he has
promised will come to pass. If you ever meet a hope-filled
person, you can bet she has mastered patience in the Lord.
The temptation is strong to become upset and impatient with
ourselves, others, and even God, but if Jesus has patience
with us in our fickle, fallen conditions, then we can learn to
exercise that same patience as well and trust that God is
going to work it all out.

ENGAGING HEAVEN

*Think of a time in your life when you recognized that God
was being patient with you. What did you learn from the
experience?*

Battle Tested

"Most assuredly, I say to you,
unless a grain of wheat falls into the ground and dies,
it remains alone; but if it dies, it produces much grain."
John 12:24 NKJV

Jesus said that unless a seed dies, it cannot produce fruit. Let me tell you, there are things in our lives that need to die. There are branches growing out of us that need to wither and dry up so God can breathe life into us and produce new, fresh fruit. If we are living just to try to feel good, we aren't going to overcome. We will never be battle tested. There are no victories without war. This is no resurrection without the cross. The Bible says, "Unless a grain of wheat falls to the ground and dies, it remains alone; but if it dies, it produces much grain." There's something about death that brings life.

ENGAGING HEAVEN

What things in your personal life do you need to let die? What is holding you back from all the new life God wants to work in you?

It Will Find You

For the wages of sin is death, but the gift of God
is eternal life in Christ Jesus our Lord.

ROMANS 6:23 NKJV

Sin still separates you from God. Yes, he paid for it on the cross, but what he paid for was your ability to be free. If you stop repenting and you don't want anything to do with the Lord, your sin will still need to be paid for. Sin has a price tag, and some people don't even bother to look at the price. The Bible says, "Take note, you have sinned against the LORD; and be sure your sin will find you out" (Numbers 32:23 NKJV). It might be years, but your sin will find you, and it will cost you because, if you live a dishonest life, God will expose it. If you think you're getting away with something, just remember that God is watching, and he cares about you too much to let it rot inside you. The Lord will warn, he'll give you a nudge, and he'll speak to your heart. If you don't listen, it's going to hurt you in the end because you're desensitizing yourself to the Holy Spirit.

ENGAGING HEAVEN

What is the Holy Spirit convicting you of?

Calling Him Faithful

By faith Sarah herself also received
strength to conceive seed,
and she bore a child when she was past the age,
because she judged Him faithful who had promised.
HEBREWS 11:11 NKJV

The truth of the Word of God overrides your feelings. The facts of the Bible are truer than how you feel. Have you been convicted by what the Bible says, or do your feelings reign supreme in your life? When Sarah was told she would have a baby, the Bible says she "laughed within herself, saying 'After I have grown old, shall I have pleasure, my lord being old also?'" (Genesis 18:12 NKJV). But in the end, Hebrews 11:11 concluded that Sarah judged that God was faithful. "Considering him faithful" is not a feeling that happens naturally; it's a deliberate decision to take time and consider who God is and what he has done. It means praising him in the storm. It means praising him even when things aren't going your way. It means remembering what God has done for us even if our feelings aren't quite there yet.

ENGAGING HEAVEN

Take some time today to reflect on the situations in your life.
Consider how he has been faithful to you.

Hope

Abraham, who is the father of us all,...
who, contrary to hope, in hope believed.

ROMANS 4:16, 18 NKJV

Earthly hope is nothing more than wishing. Unfortunately, that's all the world has to cling to and what half of the church is manifesting. Do you know what earthly hope is? It's like saying, "I hope it doesn't rain on Monday." It amounts to nothing and is powerless to actually accomplish anything. It is not going to get us very far. There's no faith in earthly hope nor action. But there is a living, active, eternal hope available to us, and often it flies in the face of earthly hope. Abraham, against all earthly wishing and worldly common sense, believed in this *real* hope because of the faith he had in God. This heavenly hope is a joyful anticipation of good, even if the world offers no indication that it is possible. We have to be agents of hope and live like people of faith. There's a storm brewing? It will pass. We don't *wish* it will pass; we *know* it will because our hope is in the Lord.

ENGAGING HEAVEN

What channel are you on? Change the channel, regroup, and receive fresh hope today.

Acts 2

"The Spirit of truth, whom the world cannot receive,
because it neither sees Him nor knows Him;
but you know Him, for He dwells with you and will be in you."

JOHN 14:17 NKJV

Pentecost was the moment when that "in you" took place,
and it empowered the early Christians to change the world.
They had an encounter with the Lord, and the outcome
of that encounter led to miracles and the spread of the
gospel—some of which is recorded in the incredible account
of Acts 2. We need an experience like Pentecost in our lives
today, but don't limit the Holy Spirit by expecting him to
only manifest at revival meetings. Acts 2 was about the Holy
Spirit empowering people to overcome in every area of their
lives. Supernatural power isn't only so you can become a
minister or a worship leader. It's so you can be a good mom
or be faithful at your job or love your neighbors. Let's stop
mystifying power and believe Romans 5:17, which says, "Much
more those who receive abundance of grace and of the gift
of righteousness will reign in life through the One, Jesus
Christ" (NKJV).

ENGAGING HEAVEN

*In what areas of your life do you need the Holy Spirit to
empower you to overcome and live like Christ?*

Pilgrimage

Blessed is the man whose strength is in You,
Whose heart is set on pilgrimage.
PSALM 84:5 NKJV

Everything these days is manufactured. The internet only shows the best of people's lives, which is at worst fake and at best selective. Mostly, it is exaggerated. The truth is that life and growth are a journey. Success isn't accidental, and it doesn't happen overnight; it's a process that takes time and intentionality. Everyone wants things done as fast as possible, but the Bible talks about the people who are blessed that set themselves on a pilgrimage. See, God gave us everything so we would live this life with our whole hearts in service to him. This is not a one-time decision but a life-long adventure. When God searches this earth to bring a great awakening, he looks for people who are willing to go the distance to fill with his power and presence. Whatever it is you feel like you're called to do, understand that it takes time.

ENGAGING HEAVEN

What are the things you need to do every single day to conquer the day, to conquer the hour, to conquer the moment?

Unsinged

We are hard-pressed on every side, yet not crushed;
we are perplexed, but not in despair;
persecuted, but not forsaken;
struck down, but not destroyed.

2 CORINTHIANS 4:8–9 NKJV

You are an overcomer. The things of earth can't touch you. Don't give the devil more credit than he's due. Don't live as if you're crushed, abandoned, or destroyed because you're not. Peter was able to walk on water when he was looking at Jesus (Matthew 14:29). That's the only way to do miracles. Have you been thrown into the fiery furnace? Don't focus on the flames. Look up and see that Jesus is still standing right beside you. The flames can't touch you. The lions can't touch you. The waves can't touch you while your eyes are on Jesus. Don't react to darkness; run to Jesus. He's in the furnace and the pit and the storm with you. He's sitting right in your boat ready to give you his perfect peace.

ENGAGING HEAVEN

Whatever you are going through today, where are your eyes? What are you focusing on?

Two Trees

Do not be deceived, God is not mocked;
for whatever a man sows, that he will also reap.

GALATIANS 6:7 NKJV

There were two trees in the garden: two choices bearing two very different consequences. Sometimes lines can seem blurred, which is why it's so important that we know what the Lord says. Whenever he says something, the devil is on the scene trying to cast doubt and mess with us. In life, we have decisions to make, and those decisions come with consequences that we have to live with. There are still two trees. There is still a right and wrong. In a world so confused about which way is up, we can always look to God and know what truth is. If the seeds we're sowing are from the evil tree, we're going to reap a lot of pain and confusion. But if we are careful to always sow seeds from the good tree, we can have confidence that God is going to grow something beautiful. Decisions matter.

ENGAGING HEAVEN

What seeds are you sowing?

Deconstructing the Gospel

[Our gospel] is veiled to those...whose minds the god of this age has blinded, who do not believe, lest the light of the gospel of the glory of Christ, who is the image of God, should shine on them.

2 CORINTHIANS 4:3-4 NKJV

Our culture attempts to portray truth as subjective. What is truth? Nobody wants to hear things they don't like anymore. That's why we've tried to deconstruct the Bible, manipulating it to fit our desired way of living instead of the other way around. But by doing so, we've created a gospel that is no longer effective. It doesn't hold any power. The truth— whether we want to hear it or not—is that God gave us a way to live, and the gospel clearly lays it out for us. The Bible says that God sent Jesus to earth as a plumb line (Amos 7:7-8), meaning he's the standard by which everything else is measured. Often when we go out to eat, we'll adjust our order, adding certain things and leaving other things out. That's fine with a salad or a coffee but certainly not with faith. The gospel is not whatever we want it to be; it is our ultimate standard for us to adjust our lives by.

ENGAGING HEAVEN

What happens when our feelings, rather than Jesus, become the standard by which we live?

Identity

So the true children of Abraham
have the same faith as their father!
GALATIANS 3:7 TPT

Your life is not defined by your pain and hurt or what you went through as a child. Your life is defined by the destiny of God in you. And when you can tap into that identity, you'll soar. The first door to shut is the opinions of others. Friends, rejected people reject others. The devil tries to use the pain of rejection to disguise your identity. Your walls come up, and you become easily angry and offended. Another painful door to shut is the door of guilt and failure. Failure isn't final, ladies. That isn't who you are. But the devil wants you to wear that as your identity. He wants you to live in the hole of your last mistake. People struggle moving forward, but it's time to close that book and start afresh because your life today matters.

ENGAGING HEAVEN

Is there someone you need to forgive? Perhaps you need to forgive yourself.

September

Exceeding the Need

God is able to make all grace abound toward you,
that you, always having all sufficiency in all things,
may have an abundance for every good work.

2 Corinthians 9:8 NKJV

The law of Moses stated that if there was a famine in that day, you had the right to return to your homeland and glean from the scraps of the fields to feed yourself. Naomi decided to go, and Ruth went with her even though Ruth was not even a Hebrew girl. As she was gathering scraps for herself and Naomi, Boaz, the owner of the field, noticed her. Although the scraps were already scarce, he told his reapers to be sloppy handed, to lay some extras down on the ground for her but not to tell her. Not only did Ruth fill all her baskets, but she ended up owning the fields when she married Boaz. God honored Ruth's loyalty to Naomi when she decided to go with her mother-in-law rather than stay and try to find a new husband. See, Ruth didn't serve a God of scraps, and neither do we.

ENGAGING HEAVEN

God wants to give you more than you deserve or could imagine! You're trying to get scraps from a field that you're about to own.

Captive Thoughts

Casting down arguments and every high thing that exalts itself against the knowledge of God, bringing every thought into captivity to the obedience of Christ...

2 CORINTHIANS 10:5 NKJV

All the little tests in life are there to prepare us for the next level. It's not the guy at work or the difficult relative who's making your life difficult. It's principalities and powers as strongholds. Our lives are ordained by the Holy Ghost, so let's live and respond to trials and tests like we actually believe it. This starts with our thoughts. Our thoughts are directed by what we surround ourselves with. Are you reading the Bible? What do you set before your eyes on the internet? What kinds of shows do you watch? Does your mind run wild, or are you taking your thoughts captive? Do you own your thoughts, or do your thoughts own you? What kind of people are you surrounded by? See, the people in our lives either feed our faith or push doubt and unbelief into our minds. Be careful who and what you listen to. The true and living Word of God has been given to us. Let's start proclaiming it over our thoughts.

ENGAGING HEAVEN

Are you confessing the Word of God?

Grounded in Love

"I will be a true Father to you,
and you will be my beloved sons and daughters,"
says the Lord Yahweh Almighty.
2 CORINTHIANS 6:18 TPT

So many people perceive God through the lens of a dad who hurt them or the person who abandoned them. They live like orphans instead of like the dearly loved sons and daughters that they are. God's love for them is real and reachable, but they don't know how to receive it. Two keys to receiving God's love are loving ourselves and loving others. Loving ourselves isn't selfish; in a balanced, godly way, it's essential. How can we receive God's love if we hate ourselves and don't believe we *should* be loved? It's time we understood what abundant love really means. Loving others matters, too, because those are God's children. How can we say we love God if we don't love his children? If we're harboring hurt, anger, or judgment, we can't love others because it blocks us. We need to pray for God's help to let those things go so we can love others, love ourselves, and receive all the love God yearns to lavishly pour out on us.

ENGAGING HEAVEN

When you look at life, is it through the lens of love or hurt?

Love, Not Acceptance

Therefore, having these promises, beloved, let us cleanse ourselves from all filthiness of the flesh and spirit, perfecting holiness in the fear of God.

2 CORINTHIANS 7:1 NKJV

Morality is at an all-time low. The lines of truth and sin have become so blurry. People don't understand the difference between love and acceptance. As Christians, we're called to love until it hurts. But acceptance means receiving what the world is selling, and that's not acceptable. Sin is still sin, and bondage is still bondage. We've weakened intimacy to casual hookups: no emotion, no love, no commitment, no spirit realm. There is obvious fruit in a believer's life, but nowadays we just walk around the planet and give in to whatever urge comes our way. It's time to love but not accept. That doesn't mean we need to throw our beliefs on other people, but we can't let them throw all their beliefs on us either. Christianity in this culture rarely looks different from the world around it. What separates us from the world? It's time we start making that separation clear.

ENGAGING HEAVEN

What is the difference between love and acceptance? How can you love someone without accepting their sin?

Focus on You

Let everyone be devoted to fulfill the work God has given them to do with excellence, and their joy will be in doing what's right and being themselves, and not in being affirmed by others.

GALATIANS 6:4 TPT

Do you judge yourself harshly? It's easy to look around and wish you had *her* life, *her* money, *her* body, *her* personality. If you don't have a strong sense of self-worth and an awareness of how much God loves you, you're going to treat yourself horribly and that is the biggest door for compromise to break into your life. We're all unique, and you're amazing. You just need to figure out how he made *you*. Stop giving your attention to all the areas you feel lacking in and recognize how you shine. Use it for God's purpose in your life. We're to prefer people. We're to love them and celebrate them. But if you're comparing yourself to others, then what you're doing is compromising the value God has for you by assigning your worth to other people's standards instead of his. You were designed for a unique purpose that nobody else can fulfill but you.

ENGAGING HEAVEN

What part do you play in the body of Christ?

A Better Way

You are of God, little children, and have overcome them, because He who is in you is greater than he who is in the world.

1 John 4:4 NKJV

There is a kingdom available to us. Jesus came to this earth to die for our sins and so that his plan could be fulfilled in us. And it wouldn't be through the sky, and it wouldn't be through looking for external circumstances, although much of Christianity is propped up that way. The kingdom would be manifest within us. When the disciples walked with Jesus, he was limited to flesh and blood. When he healed the sick, he did it as God but also as a man. He came to show us a better way. The way he lived is the way we should live. The way he thought is the way we should think. He didn't come in all his glory and power; he had a common name, and he was birthed in a common stable so that God could identify with our flesh. He proved to us that he identified with this world and showed us a better way to be. There was a King among us, and this King came to serve.

ENGAGING HEAVEN

Jesus overcame temptation so we could. He overcame death, hell, and the grave so we could. It is the hope of glory, Christ in you.

Pride Is Ugly

The twenty-four elders fall down before Him who sits on the
throne and worship Him who lives forever and ever, and cast
their crowns before the throne, saying:
"You are worthy, O Lord,
To receive glory and honor and power;
For You created all things,
And by Your will they exist and were created."
REVELATION 4:10–11 NKJV

Everybody today wants followers. They want likes, they want
to be noticed, and they're trying so hard to make a name for
themselves. But the real realms of heaven are not like that at
all. We live in a very self-centered, individualistic society, but
pride is an ugly thing. It's a trap that only leads to depression;
it doesn't lead to the cross. See, at the foot of the cross,
we're all the same. We've each been given unique gifts, but
one day we're going to lay down our gifts, along with our
crowns, at the feet of Jesus. If we're so focused on being
noticed, can we really hide in the Lord? Can we trust him and
serve him and do great things that *actually* matter without
getting caught up in the recognition? And so today, let's
focus on eternal things and not fall into the trap of thinking
too much of ourselves.

ENGAGING HEAVEN

*When all things had been given into his hands, Jesus took
a towel, knelt down, and washed his friends' feet (John
13:4–5). Are you willing to do the same?*

Love Glasses

Let nothing be done through selfish ambition or conceit,
but in lowliness of mind
let each esteem others better than himself.

PHILIPPIANS 2:3 NKJV

Instead of wearing lenses of offense, let's put on Christ's love glasses. Love glasses help us see one another differently. They help us see ourselves differently. We even see the Father differently. Instead of judging, we have a lot more grace, and we stop measuring ourselves and others with an impossible scale of perfection. In turn, we understand the love and grace of God much more clearly. There's no reason for us, as children of a loving God, to walk in shame and condemnation as if we're outside of the grace of God. Love God and treat yourself with kindness. Stop tearing yourself down and don't tear others down. That's not how God is, so it shouldn't be how we are either. If we learn to love and we learn to receive love from God, our lives will improve, and our relationships will flourish.

ENGAGING HEAVEN

Esteeming others as better than ourselves does not require self-depreciation. How can having grace and love for ourselves help us to better show grace and love for others?

Acceptance

He chose us in Him before the foundation of the world,
that we should be holy and without blame
before Him in love.
EPHESIANS 1:4 NKJV

God chose us. That means he picked you. He had you in
mind. His eyes were on you, and he chose you as his beloved
daughter. He wanted you to be his own, even before the
world was formed. He *chose* you. When you're in God's
family, you're accepted for who you are. God is not going
to be embarrassed by you because you're in his family. You
have all the family rights and privileges. As his daughter, you
have access to his name and to his unconditional love and
acceptance because you are his own. You're a Christian. You
are a believer. You are a daughter of the King. Are you living
up to it? Are you living life with no fear, walking in boldness
and courage, believing that miracles are for today? That's the
life you should expect when you are part of God's family.

ENGAGING HEAVEN

What does it mean to be "holy and without blame"?

The Danger of Isolation

Not forsaking the assembling of ourselves together,
as is the manner of some, but exhorting one another,
and so much the more as you see the Day approaching.
HEBREWS 10:25 NKJV

As Christians, our judgment is being destroyed by the isolation we put ourselves in. We were created to live in community and work together as a body of believers. Difficult times are an invitation for us to experience breakthrough, but we're not going to get there without backup, without our brothers and sisters. There is a danger in isolation, and it shows in our judgment. It is imperative that we open our eyes and recheck our priorities. Do you prioritize your relationships, most importantly your relationship with God? Or are you too focused on your own agenda to make room in your life for others. If you really want to hear God's voice, you have to turn down the volume of the world. It's time to mute the machine. Let's get back to the better work of living for the things that matter—the only things that will last. Let's live for God and for each other.

ENGAGING HEAVEN

Reach out to someone who has been on your heart. Grab coffee or lunch. Be intentional about fellowship this week.

Give It Away

"This poor widow has given a larger offering
than any of the wealthy.
For the rich only gave out of their surplus,
but she sacrificed out of her poverty
and gave to God all that she had to live on."
LUKE 21:3-4 TPT

We all make decisions: where to work, where to attend school, whom to marry, how to raise our kids, who our friends are going to be. All those things matter. But if we're not careful, our flesh can easily get in the way. That's when we start making decisions based around our "wants" instead of our "needs." God gave us choices, but in the midst of so many options, we sometimes have a hard time picking the right one. We want the blessing of the Lord and his favor in our lives, but do we know his voice? Can we hear his guidance? When we understand his absolutes and *his* desires, that will help guide our decisions instead of letting our flesh call the shots. Let's decide to live our lives for the glory of God and for what the Lord wants us to do. There is a way God wants us to live, and when we follow his perfect path, everything we could ever imagine will be given to us.

ENGAGING HEAVEN

It's a really hard concept to grasp, but when we give it all up for God, he gives it all back...but better.

Posture Matters

Always be eager to present yourself before God
as a perfect and mature minister, without shame,
as one who correctly explains the Word of Truth.
2 Timothy 2:15 TPT

Fear has a posture. Worry, concern, and lack have a posture.
When a child is disciplined, you can see her shoulders shrink
and face fall downward. Now, children tend to bounce back
up, but some people hold that posture for years. In every
relationship, they feel insecure and unworthy. How many
people buy into a lie that they're somehow lacking? They
lack love, joy, confidence, self-esteem. They believe they're
never going to amount to anything. Lack is a mindset that
tries to hold people down. The enemy delights in seeing us in
a posture of being slumped over and defeated. But there's a
different posture God wants us to have: the feeling of being
free, unhindered, and unrestrained. How do you think that
posture would look? Probably threatening to the enemy and
welcoming to a world locked up in lies. Psalm 3:3 tells us that
God lifts our heads. *That* is the posture he intends for you, his
beloved daughter in whom he delights.

ENGAGING HEAVEN

What posture are you in?

Accomplishing So Little

Don't allow your hearts to grow dull or lose your enthusiasm, but follow the example of those who fully received what God has promised because of their strong faith and patient endurance.

HEBREWS 6:12 TPT

What are you believing for? Do you feel like you're accomplishing so little with the time you've been given? What are you investing in? There is no middle ground: you're either wasting your life watching television and allowing social media to direct your narrative, or you're putting your time toward what God has laid on your heart. Are you just trying to coast through life? Or are you dreaming, writing, creating, praying, and doing things for God? Saying no to easy pleasures and investing in the long game will pay off. You will come out of it stronger than ever before, with greater faith and greater power because you invested in the work of God, and he will continue to invest in you. There is so much he wants to accomplish, and you are his chosen vessel.

ENGAGING HEAVEN

Are you busy doing nothing, or are you acting in faith?

Drowning Out the Noise

This world and its desires are in the process of passing away,
but those who love to do the will of God live forever.

1 JOHN 2:17 TPT

Nothing in the world can satisfy your longing for God except
fellowship with him. It's those forbidden cravings of the world
that drown out the voice of the Lord. The world makes it very
easy for us to fill our ears and eyes with all types of things
other than God. It's like the enemy is a perpetual sound
machine. The devil wants it to be so normal to not hear
God. The Lord's there. Somewhere on the other side of this
noisy life is God, and the devil doesn't want you to hear him.
Of course, he's always there, but we push him far into the
background of our lives. The day is coming for every person
when only God will remain. Everything else in this life will
pass away, and when it does, God will be there. Don't make
that the day you try to get acquainted with him.

ENGAGING HEAVEN

*Bitterness and offense can drown out the Lord. Media can
drown him out. Even your hobbies cannot come before
hearing the voice of your Father. What sound do you need to
turn down in your life?*

Faith Requires Relationship

Behold, I'm standing at the door, knocking.
If your heart is open to hear my voice
and you open the door within,
I will come in to you and feast with you,
and you will feast with me.

REVELATION 3:20 TPT

Lazarus was dead. Lazarus was somebody Jesus knew and loved. He had a relationship with Jesus. Lazarus was the brother of Mary and Martha (John 11:5–16). People were moved by grief and stirred in their faith by his death because they loved Lazarus. See, faith requires relationship. People want to operate in faith, but they don't realize the relationships that need to be cultivated first. God is not a get-out-of-jail-free card. We can't expect God to move through us if we're unwilling to cultivate a relationship with him. In Matthew 9:36, while Jesus was preaching and teaching, he looked upon the crowd and realized that they were like sheep without a shepherd. They were lost and wayward. So, what he did was turn to those closest to him and commissioned them to heal the sick, cleanse the lepers, and raise the dead. He was ready to act out in faith, and to do so, he chose to use his closest friends.

ENGAGING HEAVEN

Are you cultivating a daily relationship with God so that when he's ready to move, he turns and looks at you?

Killing Comparison

I'm not telling you this because I'm in need,
for I have learned to be satisfied in any circumstance.
PHILIPPIANS 4:11 TPT

The apostle Paul had been imprisoned, stoned, and shipwrecked. Yet while he was in literal chains, he wrote a letter to the Philippians that included this verse. No matter what his circumstances were, he found contentment in the love of his Lord. If Paul were alive today, I don't think he'd be jealous of the online photo dump of someone else's vacation. He wouldn't be worried about a fake Instagram pic or fight for "likes" by uploading a dozen selfies a day. Paul was content in who God called him to be. Even when his own life was playing out like a terrible drama, he found his identity and his peace in the Lord and his concern was for the people of the church he served. God is worthy of praise, regardless of how your life is unfolding. Satan will try to pull your focus off God and onto your own "shipwrecks," and he'll win that battle if you're constantly comparing yourself to others. What has God called *you* to?

ENGAGING HEAVEN

When you feel the temptation to compare yourself to others, how can you find your identity in God and then serve others? Can you celebrate the successes of others instead of caving to jealousy?

The Battle Is His

You can do your best to prepare for the battle,
but ultimate victory comes from the Lord God.

PROVERBS 21:31 TPT

The Bible says, "He who is in you is greater than he who is in the world" (1 John 4:4 NKJV). Well, "he who is in the world" is the devil. God wants us to know that the battle isn't ours; it's God's. Stop worrying, stop listening to the wisdom of the flesh, and stop allowing your mind to become confused. Instead, start accepting the victory that he already assured us. We are overcomers in him. The Bible also says, "Now to Him who is able to do exceedingly abundantly above all that we ask or think, according to the power that works in us" (Ephesians 3:20 NKJV). So, our hope is within us. It's hard to understand because we live in a world that wants us to keep reaching for external things, but the kingdom is within us. We are his bride, the church. It's not a building. It's us.

ENGAGING HEAVEN

The ultimate plan of God was to live in us, that the Holy Spirit would dwell in us. Have you given him your battles and accepted his victory?

Staying Beautiful

Restore to me the joy of Your salvation,
And uphold me by Your generous Spirit.

PSALM 51:12 NKJV

Whatever difficult thing you're going through right now, it's going to end. But Jesus' love will never end. He's the only one who never changes, so keep your focus on him and you will get through this season of life. We are only as strong as what we're focused on. There are people so focused on their trials that they wear them on their faces. They live their whole life as a reaction to their trials. Don't you want to be recognized as a woman who has stayed beautiful on the outside and the inside? Let the joy of Christ light up your countenance and restore your joy every morning. His goodness will prove better at making you beautiful than any skin care regimen. Hurricanes of trial come and go in life, but they can't destroy your joy or beauty if Jesus is your anchor and your Rock.

ENGAGING HEAVEN

Joy is the first thing the enemy wants to steal, but God wants to restore it in your life today. How can you work with the Lord to restore joy in your life?

Many Turn Away

The Holy Spirit has explicitly revealed: At the end of this age,
many will depart from the true faith one after another,
devoting themselves to spirits of deception
and following demon-inspired revelations and theories.
Hypocritical liars will deceive many,
and their consciences won't bother them at all!

1 TIMOTHY 4:1-2 TPT

Certain doctrines are killing Christianity as we know it. But
a remnant of people is stopping, watching, praying, and
holding fast to truth. They're the ones who have stayed
close to God, who know what his Word says, and whose
consciences are still sensitive to the nudging of the Holy
Spirit. Paul warns that those who turn away have seared their
conscience. They're not listening to their Father anymore,
and instead, they are following the wisdom of the world. But
the thing about truth is that even when it's not popular, it's
still true. This is not a religious set of standards but knowing
who God is and what he has said. That's where peace can be
found. That's where joy lies. That's true, holy living—not by
my standards or your friends' standards but the standards of
your Father in heaven.

ENGAGING HEAVEN

*How can you keep your conscience sensitive in a world bent
on hardening your heart?*

Anchored in God

This hope we have as an anchor of the soul,
both sure and steadfast,
and which enters the Presence behind the veil.

HEBREWS 6:19 NKJV

Some people, especially mothers and grandmothers, are exceptionally caring and nurturing. This is a great gift, but if they're not careful, they can end up taking on too much responsibility and going into crisis mode. How many moms start out fired up, excited, eager to raise great kids, but they have their first baby and suddenly forget all about themselves? The love they feel becomes mixed up with concern, anxiety, and guilt. They forget what made them great and who assigned them the role of mother. Some grandmothers become so caught up in family emergencies that they lose their sweetness and their stability. If we're going to be effective in whatever God has called us to do, we cannot lose our stability. We must remain anchored in God and in the truth of his Word. It's God's desire for us that we remain strong and stable in him, and he will help us overcome anything we're up against.

ENGAGING HEAVEN

When crisis hits, do you become flustered or remain steadfast in God?

Have Patience

Let patience have its perfect work,
that you may be perfect and complete,
lacking nothing.

JAMES 1:4 NKJV

How many of us have asked the Lord to change us? But did we have any idea what we were signing up for? We want God to change us quickly, and while change is inevitable, it's not a quick fix. It's a process. What we really need is to be patient and faithful while we stay poised to receive what he has for us. If we fail to develop patience, it will block the work God is trying to do because we give up and become discouraged too quickly. We are on a journey of sanctification with our Lord, and it's not all going to be completed today. In fact, what often happens shortly after we ask the Lord to change us is that we face opposition. Why? Because that is part of the changing process. How will we change if our circumstances never do? So, the first step to real, lasting change is to develop patience—because we're going to need it.

ENGAGING HEAVEN

How can you exercise patience while God works through you to change and grow you?

And Then Some

Put your heart and soul into every activity you do,
as though you are doing it for the Lord himself
and not merely for others.

COLOSSIANS 3:23 TPT

In Genesis 24, we see a love story. Abraham's son, Isaac, was looking for a girl, so Abraham sent Eliezer to find Isaac a wife. Now, Eliezer wasn't sure how to find a girl, but he had ten camels with him. He came up with a plan to sit by a well because that was where women gathered. Eliezer wanted a wife for Isaac who was beautiful, kind, and then some. So, he prayed and asked God for a girl who, when Eliezer asked for a drink of water, would offer to water his camels as well. By God's faithfulness, Rebekah came along. She did all that Eliezer asked and then some. Like Rebekah, we should also go above and beyond. Go the extra mile. Be faithful. Keep your word. Do what God has called you to do. Let your "yes be yes" and follow through. As Christians, we need to form a culture of diligence. It isn't enough to simply want to "get by" because we serve an abundant God who is more than enough and then some.

ENGAGING HEAVEN

How can you go above and beyond in your faithfulness to God today?

God Provides

Casting all your care upon Him,
for He cares for you.
1 PETER 5:7 NKJV

Who is our provider? Is it God or people? Is it the Father or
the paycheck? The Lord said there is one thing he wants
us to concern ourselves with, and he would take care of
the rest. He said, "Seek first the kingdom of God and His
righteousness, and all these things shall be added to you"
(Matthew 6:33 NKJV). Life gives us a lot of worries: bills,
marriage, children, school, work. We're bogged down with so
many responsibilities. We even worry about things that will
never happen. But worrying is inherently demonic, and the
enemy is knocking. He will take every inch of our minds that
we let him occupy. It's time to evict him and cast our cares on
God. There are workers, and there are worshipers. Between
the two, worshipers will always end up getting more done.

ENGAGING HEAVEN

What cares are you carrying around today?

Covenant

Without faith it is impossible to please Him,
for he who comes to God must believe that He is,
and that He is a rewarder of those who diligently seek Him.
HEBREWS 11:6 NKJV

For us to come to God, the Bible says we "must believe that
He is." He's what? Everything. If you come to God, you must
believe that he's your healer. He's your provider. He's your
deliverer. He's your friend. He's the revelator. He's the burning
one. He's the all-consuming fire. He is Jehovah Jireh. He is
our protector. Those who come to God must believe that *he
is* and that he will reward us when we seek him diligently.
I'm not saying go on a two-year journey like the wise men.
I'm not saying give up your life when you meet Jesus like
Simeon. But you do need to re-covenant. Consider the
covenants of God and how they have influenced your faith
and your decisions.

ENGAGING HEAVEN

What are some of the promises God has made to you?

Too Grateful to Complain

Live a cheerful life, without complaining or division among
yourselves. For then you will be seen as innocent, faultless,
and pure children of God, even though you live in the midst
of a brutal and perverse culture. For you will appear among
them as shining lights in the universe.

PHILIPPIANS 2:14–15 TPT

The world feeds us criticism and complaint. It's not hard to
find faults in the church, in our jobs, in one another, in our
spouses, even in our kids. The enemy is so good at pushing
negativity to be our agenda, but children of God think
differently than everybody else. We act differently than
everybody else. We live in a realm of hope and love, not
despairing, because we trust that God has us, and not judging
because we know we have been graciously forgiven. The Lord
isn't shocked by what you're going through. He's not shocked
by your disappointments. As his children, we are able to
stand on his Word and live with the greatest hope ever. When
that happens, criticism crumbles away, and we're filled with
a contagious gratefulness. So, the next time you go through
something rough, rejoice. Start praising God if you go through
the valley of the shadow of death, and start getting excited
when trials come. God is going to move on your behalf.

ENGAGING HEAVEN

*God is your deliverer. God is your defender. He wants to
fill you with the kind of unexplainable peace that will be a
testimony to others. Go to him with your trials today.*

Proof Providers

Love has been perfected among us in this:
that we may have boldness in the day of judgment;
because as He is, so are we in this world.
1 JOHN 4:17 NKJV

If we study the Bible long enough, guess what? The world's craziness and confusion diminish from our lives. Renewed minds are what prove the will of God. When we believe lies and tolerate the world's chaos, it ends up hurting us and affecting our spiritual walk. No, we don't have to accept everything. The ever-praised value of acceptance does not need to include sin or demons or moral compromise. Our godly standard of living needs to return, and it's not going to be reestablished through one devotional. It's going to require renewing our minds through discipline and consistency and proving God's will by obeying his Word. We should not be looking to the world for an example of authenticity: that's found in the Bible. The world cannot give us a reliable moral compass, but as we behold Jesus, we are delivered from the confusion and set on a straight course. We are the proof providers of the Word of God.

ENGAGING HEAVEN

"As he is, so are we." Who is he? He is strong, complete, loving, and unwavering.

I Will Remember

I pray for you that the faith we share may effectively deepen your understanding of every good thing that belongs to you in Christ.

PHILEMON 1:6 TPT

King Jehoshaphat faced a battle far too great for him. He was scared, so the first thing he did was "set himself to seek the LORD" (2 Chronicles 20:3 NKJV). Immediately, he calls for a fast, starts praying, and cries out to God for help. There's no way he can win in this battle in the natural. But he reminded himself of how God had already delivered him in the past. There will be times when life is too hard for us to overcome by ourselves, and those are the moments when we need to recall the great things God has done. It's imperative that we remember. We don't give testimony for God's sake; God doesn't need to be reminded of what he's done. We need it. And when you remember what God has done in your life, that is the key to breakthrough. That is the key to defeating fear and seeing through the enemy's lies.

ENGAGING HEAVEN

When God does something great in your life, make a note of it either in your Bible or in a journal. One day, you will need to be reminded of it.

Angels on Assignment

Then the LORD opened the eyes of the young man,
and he saw.
And behold, the mountain was full of horses
and chariots of fire all around Elisha.
2 KINGS 6:17 NKJV

People tend to act a little skittish when the topic of angels is brought up. However, angels are real, and they're here. There's a scriptural pattern revealing them working with the Father to accomplish his will on earth. He commands his angels to guard us (Psalm 91:11), to bring us messages (Luke 1:11-13; Matthew 1:20-21, 28:5-7), and to minister to us (Hebrews 1:14). See, God cares about even the little things in your life. It may be a phone call you're waiting for or a grocery bill that ran high. Regardless of how trivial things in your life may seem, God cares about them because he cares about you. He sees everything and knows everything. He cares about every little detail regarding you, and he is never far away.

ENGAGING HEAVEN

How does it make you feel knowing that your Father has the army of heaven at his disposal and he's committed to caring for you?

Obedience

Though He was a Son, yet He learned obedience
by the things which He suffered.
HEBREWS 5:8 NKJV

If Christ had to learn obedience, we definitely have some
work to do. It might not be easy, but it is going to be worth
it. Obedience is everything. We are called to invade this
earth with the gospel, with God's power, with his boldness.
Everybody wants power, but power is with a purpose. We are
not going to receive the power of God without the purpose
of God. So, if God gave you all power and all authority, what
would you do with it? Do you know what your purpose is?
Do you have an idea of what you want to do for the gospel
to see this world changed? That is the difference between
simply reading his words and obeying what he said. True
obedience leads to a life of supernatural power. It is power
with a purpose.

ENGAGING HEAVEN

*We are called to bring heaven to earth. What are some
attributes of heaven that you exemplify in your life?*

Healthy Fear

Therefore, my beloved, as you have always obeyed,
not as in my presence only, but now much more in my
absence, work out your own salvation with fear and
trembling.

PHILIPPIANS 2:12 NKJV

Do you know what we don't see much of today? A healthy
fear of God. Serving the King means we operate by a
different set of rules. We're not God. Therefore, there will be
rules and standards that we may not like, but we obey them
anyway. We say no to the things of this earth to embrace a
heavenly calling. There needs to be a healthy fear and awe
of our Creator in each of us because that will compel us to
live right. This is not a fear of just going to hell because that's
not really the point of the gospel. This fear is a convicting
reverence for the one who made it all and holds us all in
his hands. We're going to continually be frustrated if we're
calling ourselves Christians and yet living according to our
own set of rules. On the other hand, "The fear of the LORD is
the beginning of wisdom" (Proverbs 9:10 NKJV).

ENGAGING HEAVEN

Are you working things out with trembling?

October

Lessons from the Desert

They could not enter in
because of unbelief.
HEBREWS 3:19 NKJV

If asked, "What are some examples of evil?" What would
you answer? Probably murder, rape, or adultery, right? Do
you know what the Lord calls evil? Unbelief. The Israelites
always seemed to wrestle with unbelief, to the point where
Paul used them as an example to warn us, "Today, if you will
hear His voice, do not harden your hearts as in the rebellion"
(vv. 7–8 NKJV). He referred to a portion of the Israelites'
wilderness wandering as "the rebellion." What started out as
a journey of healing and promise turned into a rebellion and
forty years of wandering around in the desert, all because
of their unbelief. He went on to warn them clearly, "Beware,
brethren, lest there be in any of you an evil heart of unbelief
in departing from the living God" (v. 12 NKJV). Today, as in
the time of the Israelites and as in the time of Paul, God is
leading you to something great, and you have the choice to
either rebel or prosper.

ENGAGING HEAVEN

Why is unbelief so evil?

Engaged in Warfare

If we died with Him, We shall also live with Him.
If we endure, We shall also reign with Him.
If we deny Him, He also will deny us.

2 TIMOTHY 2:11–12 NKJV

Are you a soldier, or are you a civilian? If you actually are in the military, you have already made your choice regarding this world and your country. As a believer, you have a similar choice to make in the spiritual realm. Make the choice of what you are going to be then act like it. Paul said that "No one engaged in warfare entangles himself with the affairs of this life" (v. 4 NKJV). Soldiers aren't worried about trite, little issues because their focus is on things much bigger and more daunting. They're on the front lines of battle fighting for lives. Instead of following their own feelings and desires, they're following the commanding officer. The Bible says that the enemy wants to steal, kill, and destroy you (John 10:10), and that's a lot easier to do if you're distracted or asleep. Paul told Timothy to "endure hardship" (v. 3) because the commanding officer he is serving is Jesus Christ. The affairs of this world are not worth all our attention and devotion, but Jesus is. He is worth all our loyalty and all the persevering required.

ENGAGING HEAVEN

What issues are you engaged with today?
What occupies your mind?

Sleeping Giant

Yes, God raised Jesus to life!
And since God's Spirit of Resurrection lives in you,
he will also raise your dying body to life
by the same Spirit that breathes life into you!
ROMANS 8:11 TPT

The greatest sleeping giant in the world is the church. Jesus paid a monumental price by dying on the cross, and he wants to empower us to overcome. But what are we overcoming? Today, Jesus no longer walks on this earth. He now lives inside of us, but that doesn't guarantee he's going to shine through. That just means he gave us the framework for the miraculous, to be full of supernatural power, and to operate in his power and might. But are we doing so? Our world is constantly looking for help externally. We have been to more conferences and revival meetings than ever, but we get less done. There are more available teachings on the Word of God but less fruit on earth than ever. We're failing to tap into the Spirit within. The greatest power on earth lives in us, and when we understand that we really *can* do everything God has called us to do, that's when we move mountains.

ENGAGING HEAVEN

Have you ever been daunted by a large mission from God? Be encouraged, knowing that he assigned it to you because he's given you everything you need. The power is already inside you.

He Is a Rewarder

Let us not grow weary while doing good,
for in due season we shall reap if we do not lose heart.
GALATIANS 6:9 NKJV

Hebrews 11:6 outlines two foundations of faith. First, we need to know who he is, and second, we need to believe that he rewards those who seek him. We give God honor and obey him because it's the right thing to do, and with that comes rewards. The rewards are not our motivation, but it's important that we recognize and celebrate that God is a rewarder. That's the reality of who he is and how he runs his kingdom. It's fundamental to faith. Even if we don't see a harvest right away, there will be growth and rewards from the good seeds we're sowing. If we don't believe that, it's we who will lose out. See, our response matters. We're rewarded for seeking, being diligent, and enduring. Believe it because our God is *that* good, and he wants us to expect his rewards.

ENGAGING HEAVEN

What are some of the ways God rewards diligent seeking?

Just Jesus

Pray without ceasing.

1 Thessalonians 5:17 NKJV

Having an opinion is fine, but when we live habitually reacting and responding out of the flesh, it will ultimately land us in a dark place. It's not healthy. How often do we ask God's opinion on decisions anymore? Do we live in a place of prayer, with open communication constantly with our Father? We live in a reactionary culture that lives on gut responses and not the wisdom God offers. When God tells you to do something, do that. Don't try to move on to the next thing when you're not finished with the last thing he's called you to do. Be careful who's speaking into your life. Just because someone is a spiritual authority doesn't mean he or she is the one God has for you. Prayer comes first. Influence can be misleading, but we need godly influence to stand. Therefore, we must have discernment and open our eyes and have an active prayer life. Everything must be filtered through the Bible and through prayer.

ENGAGING HEAVEN

If God has spoken something to you, don't be dissuaded by a contrary word, regardless of how alluring and righteous it sounds.

Dump Leah

"Nevertheless I have this against you,
that you have left your first love."
REVELATION 2:4 NKJV

Sometimes life throws you something with a catch, just like Laban did to Jacob. Jacob loved Rachel, served seven years for her hand in marriage, went to bed, woke up, and discovered his new wife was...Leah. She was *not* the one whom he had waited seven years for. In this story, Leah represents less. Not the best. Leah is dead religion. Leah is survival. Now Jacob had to decide: Would he settle for a life with Leah or embrace the hard task of serving another seven years for his true love, Rachel? Perhaps you woke up with something you didn't desire. Perhaps life has been unfair. Most people settle and give up on what they know God has called them to because of the cost. Most people are sleeping with Leah. They're not pursuing the best in life. How badly do you want "Rachel"? How long are you willing to serve and wait for God's best even when life throws you unfair curveballs? We each have the choice to either make excuses and settle or strive for God's best and never give up.

ENGAGING HEAVEN

What are you willing to pay?

Frontlines

Every soldier called to active duty must divorce
himself from the distractions of this world
so that he may fully satisfy the one who chose him.
2 TIMOTHY 2:4 TPT

Soldiers on the front lines of battle are not concerned with anything other than the fight they are engaged in. It's easy to see where people are in the battle of the Lord by what they're focused on. If they're losing their mind because someone cut them off in traffic or took their parking spot, they're probably not too worried about reaching lost souls around them or claiming ground for the Lord. Friends, we need to do better than that. We need to focus on what matters and act like we would if we were on the frontlines of battle—because we are. The world is our workplace and trivial annoyances are not worth our time or effort. When a loved one dies, we often become more focused on eternity for a time. Well, eternity doesn't change; only our perspective and mood does. We need to lock our eyes on eternity and realize that the main thing *must* be the main thing. Christ is the only mountain worth dying on.

ENGAGING HEAVEN

What are you concerning yourself with in the midst of this spiritual battle?

Make a List

Keep your thoughts continually fixed
on all that is authentic and real,
honorable and admirable, beautiful and respectful,
pure and holy, merciful and kind.
And fasten your thoughts on every glorious
work of God, praising him always.

PHILIPPIANS 4:8 TPT

Make a list of all the good things God has given you. Make a list of all the ways God has protected you and provided for you. Take some time to realize how good he has been to you. Even our health is a gift. Perhaps you're a disciplined, healthy eater. Nevertheless, you still can't eat perfect enough to earn good health because health and life come from God. Look into your life and distinguish what is noble, what is trustworthy, and what is of good report and think about these things. It's so easy to become consumed with the negative things in life, so choose to find something today to thank God for. Thank him for always being there and leading you through, even when times are tough. Whatever is going on in your life today, take a moment to make a list, think about the blessings you've received, and meditate on his goodness. Your situation will turn around.

ENGAGING HEAVEN

Take some time this week to make a list.

Grandma's Cooking

The Lord is not late with his promise to return, as some measure lateness. But rather, his "delay" simply reveals his loving patience toward you, because he does not want any to perish but all to come to repentance.

2 PETER 3:9 TPT

Do you know why everyone goes crazy for "Grandma's cooking," but nobody is screaming the praises of the "Single-girl-in-the-dorm-room's cooking"? Experience. Time. Grandma has had many, many more years to get her recipes just right. And like Grandma's cooking, Christianity can't be rushed. Christianity isn't a microwave; it's a slow cooker. It's very laborious and often mundane. It requires being faithful every day, spending time with the Lord and reading the Bible. As we do so, we'll begin to see God breaking through in powerful ways and in his perfect timing. There are amazing things on the horizon for those who are willing to stay the course. Some people receive a prophetic word, and they expect to walk out the back door of the church and take a fast track to the miraculous, but that's not how this works. Don't stop praying or believing or cooking. It takes time to master the kitchen, and faith is no different.

ENGAGING HEAVEN

Christianity isn't a sprint. It's a marathon, and we're all running to receive the prize (1 Corinthians 9:24). Are you winded already, or are you finding a good pace?

Every Blessing

His divine power has given to us all things that pertain to life and godliness, through the knowledge of Him who called us by glory and virtue.

2 Peter 1:3 NKJV

A lack of awareness of everything God has given us is crippling the church today. When you don't understand it's yours, how can you thirst for it? First Corinthians 3:21 says, "Therefore let no one boast in men. For all things are yours" (NKJV). So, how would you live differently if you realized everything were yours? Everything you need will be given to you to complete your assignment. You may not have all the talents that someone else has, but we all have something, and God has given us everything we need. We have each been given according to our abilities—or perhaps more accurately, according to our *availability*. He has already paid for every blessing; we just have to receive them as his children. Be mindful that the enemy wants to give you a mindset of "lack." Instead, claim a mindset of blessing and inheritance.

ENGAGING HEAVEN

How can you be a good steward of what God has given you?

Influence

You were once darkness,
but now you are light in the Lord.
Walk as children of light.
Ephesians 5:8 NKJV

Having discernment is vital in this world today where there
are so many people trying to mislead you. Do you recognize
that there are people with ill motives who try to influence
you to do, say, or be something for their own benefit—not
yours? That is why having discernment is so important. So,
where can we obtain godly discernment? It comes from
having a relationship with God and being influenced by him.
How we think and what we believe are going to be influenced
by outside factors, so let's make sure we're influenced by
the truth instead of the world. That's when you'll get that
little voice inside you, warning you, "This doesn't feel right."
Be careful who you're allowing to speak into your life. Just
because someone holds a position of spiritual authority does
not mean he or she is the ultimate authority. We must always
go to God for direction and truth and influence.

ENGAGING HEAVEN

*Read Ephesians 5:6–10. What are some examples
of empty words?*

Heavenly Promotions

Blessed be the God and Father of our Lord Jesus Christ,
who has blessed us with every spiritual blessing
in the heavenly places in Christ.

Ephesians 1:3 NKJV

A lot of people are self-appointed. They haven't been promoted by the Father; they promoted themselves. Now they have to work hard to maintain their image. But when God opens a door, we can rest assured knowing that he is the one who holds it open. When the Father moves in your life, you won't have to strive to make it happen. You won't have to force it or fake it. It is just there. Our success and promotion come from a place of resting in him—from a place of belief. Sitting and resting with God doesn't mean we aren't doing anything. It's actually the opposite. It means taking an active place of believing but not striving. When you know what's yours, you don't have to fight to earn it. That is the whole point of resting in the Lord.

ENGAGING HEAVEN

Read all of Ephesians 1 and consider what God wants you to do and what he has promised he will do.

Feelings

Whenever our hearts make us feel guilty and remind us of our failures, we know that God is much greater and more merciful than our conscience, and he knows everything there is to know about us.

1 JOHN 3:20 TPT

When Jacob's dad, Isaac, was on his deathbed, Jacob faked being Esau in order to steal Esau's blessing as the firstborn son. Jacob wore goatskin on his arms so when Isaac felt him, his father concluded, "The voice is Jacob's voice, but the hands are the hands of Esau" (Genesis 27:22 NKJV). He went by what he felt and not by what he heard, and therefore, he was deceived. See, we fall prey to trusting in our feelings. Our feelings will lead us astray if that's the only thing we're leaning on. Our emotions are as untrustworthy as Jacob's were. Regardless of how we feel, we need to listen to the voice of God and trust what we know is right. If it feels right and the Bible says it's wrong, it's wrong. The best way to not become deceived is to study the Scriptures and to know the voice of the Lord personally.

ENGAGING HEAVEN

Are you led by your feelings or by the Word of God?

Love Walk

Put on tender mercies, kindness,
humility, meekness, longsuffering;
bearing with one another, and forgiving one another...
even as Christ forgave you, so you also must do.
But above all these things put on love,
which is the bond of perfection.

COLOSSIANS 3:12–14 NKJV

Just as there are warning lights in our cars, God gives us warning lights in our relationships, and it's imperative that we pay attention to them. Some warning signs are thoughts like, *Why does this person cause a reaction in me?* or *Why do I feel this way?* We can't control how people respond or react, but we can control how we love. Sometimes we need to forgive people in our hearts even if they never asked for forgiveness. And the very people whom we may be trying to get out of our life, God likely put there as a test for us to pass. Instead of trying to find new, low-maintenance friends, let's be faithful to the relationships we've been given. It's a love walk. Relationships require maintenance, care, attention, and plenty of forgiveness. This is especially true within a marriage. Love fuels relationships.

ENGAGING HEAVEN

Are you struggling to love someone today? How does Jesus' life encourage you in your relationships?

Down the Mountain

I have fought the good fight,
I have finished the race,
I have kept the faith.
2 Timothy 4:7 NKJV

It's not how you start, but it's how you finish. Being faithful is important. When you die, you're going to be remembered for how you finished your life. Few people will remember how you started. You're not going to receive any accolades for running really hard at the beginning of the track. It's all about how you finish. Moses went up a mountain to meet with God, but then he came back down to deliver God's message to the Israelites. What if he had not come back down? What if he had gotten so caught up on the mountain that he didn't finish his assignment? Friends, we become so fixated on climbing our own personal mountains, but what are you going to do with the experience? If we don't make wise moves, plan our descents, and complete our assignments, we're living like fools. The top of the mountain is great, but don't get stuck there. Think ahead and finish strong.

ENGAGING HEAVEN

Why is it important to come back down the mountain?

The Rewarder

We know that we will receive a reward
an inheritance from the Lord,
as we serve the Lord Yahweh, the Anointed One!
Colossians 3:24 TPT

It is a mockery of God to think that we're going to seek his face and go after him and that he won't reward us. It is a mockery to think that we're going to sow into the Spirit and not reap a reward for it. If we have the mindset that everybody needs an equal share, we will struggle with people in the faith who have more than we do: more faith, more finances, more opportunities, perhaps more influence. We'll become frustrated and wonder why we're not blessed as much or in the same way as they are. The parable of the talents makes many people feel uneasy. Of course, we seek the Giver rather than the gift, but we cannot and *should not* ignore the fact that our God is a generous God who loves to reward his children. It's unbiblical and imbalanced to ignore that. What's the effect when we "Seek first the kingdom of God and His righteousness"? That's right: "All these things shall be added to you" (Matthew 6:33 NKJV). Our God loves to reward!

ENGAGING HEAVEN

*What rewards has God given you for your faith
and diligence?*

Grab a Towel

Then he poured water into a basin
and began to wash the disciples' dirty feet
and dry them with his towel.

JOHN 13:5 TPT

Jesus was nearing the end of his life; he knew that it was ending soon. He also knew that God had given him everything. There was probably a sense of graduation and accomplishment. The Bible says that Jesus realized that all things were given to him and that the end was near. What a powerful statement! He was finishing this race of coming to earth as a man, and he had everything he could ever want. The finality and totality of it is incredible. So, with this knowledge, what does he do? What would *you* do? This is like your Oscar speech. You've accomplished what you set out to do, and the stage is yours. Jesus went in front of the disciples, everybody was watching, and he bent down, grabbed a towel, and began to wash their dirty feet. Wait, what? Jesus chose to serve. That was the purpose of his life. What is the purpose of yours?

ENGAGING HEAVEN

Whom are you serving?

People Pleasing

Do I now persuade men, or God?
Or do I seek to please men?
For if I still pleased men,
I would not be a bondservant of Christ.

GALATIANS 1:10 NKJV

People are scared of other people. Fear of man is a huge thing. If we're so scared of what others are going to think about us, then most of our decisions will not be based on pleasing God; they'll be based on pleasing a person. We're not here to make sure everybody likes us; we're here to obey God unto death. The Bible says Jesus grew in favor with God and man (Luke 2:52), and our problem is that we try to reverse that order by growing in favor with man and then God. It should be the exact opposite. When we get favor with God, winning the favor of people will follow afterward. They'll hate us and love us, just like they did Jesus. So, the most important thing is grabbing hold of what the Lord has for us and seeking his face first.

ENGAGING HEAVEN

Do you try your best to please God even if it's unpopular?

Insta-Lonely

If we walk in the light as He is in the light,
we have fellowship with one another,
and the blood of Jesus Christ His Son
cleanses us from all sin.

1 John 1:7 NKJV

There is a horrible epidemic of depression and loneliness on this earth right now, and it is at levels that we have never seen. In this age of technology and social media, it's the most unsocial time we've ever lived in. We should be connecting to the world, conquering territories, and doing great things for God, but we're just lonely. This is directly connected to a lack of intimacy, prayer, and relationship with God and with one another. The Father said, "Where two or three are gathered together in My name, I am there in the midst of them" (Matthew 18:20 NKJV). Why? Because people matter. Fellowship matters. There is safety in a multitude of counselors (Proverbs 11:14). We were made for relationships with God and with each other, and when we don't pursue these or prioritize them, loneliness is bound to set in.

ENGAGING HEAVEN

How, specifically, are you prioritizing your relationships today?

First Class Faith

Who is he who overcomes the world,
but he who believes that Jesus is the Son of God?

1 John 5:5 NKJV

As people of faith, there shouldn't be areas in our lives where we've already given up and stopped believing that God can turn them around. How do we know what God will and won't do? Just because it has taken a long time doesn't mean he has forgotten. Have you given up on ever finding a spouse? Conceiving a child? Seeing a loved one saved? Being happy? Operating in the supernatural? Is one of your dreams to make a lot of money so you can support orphanages for the kingdom? Whatever it is that has been placed in your heart, don't settle for a place below where God has called you to live—even if it takes time. If we're going to have first class faith and soar above mediocrity, we need to overcome the roadblocks in our minds first. Believing for something miraculous isn't absurd for people of faith. It's actually needed.

ENGAGING HEAVEN

What dreams are you holding on to? What steps are you taking to achieve them?

Control

Humble yourselves under the mighty hand of God,
that He may exalt you in due time.
1 Peter 5:6 NKJV

The big lie is that God is in control. That's not true. God is in *charge*, but you're in control. And one of the hardest things to do in life is relinquish back to him the control he has given you. But do you know what's even harder? *Not* giving God control of your life and striving hard every day to make it in your own strength. We are vessels the Lord wants to work through. He gives us control to do what we want, but the best decision we can make for our lives is to humbly submit to his better way. Then, instead of striving and straining, we allow God to lead us and exalt us in his perfect time. So, to be effective, to be a light that shines in a dark world, to find breakthrough in this season, let's relinquish our control to the one who knows best.

ENGAGING HEAVEN

When you go through difficult times, do you consciously give God control? Stop and say, Okay, God, what are you trying to do in my heart through this? I'm giving you the control.

Marriage

Do not be unequally yoked together with unbelievers.
For what fellowship has righteousness with lawlessness?
And what communion has light with darkness?

2 CORINTHIANS 6:14 NKJV

It's just as easy to marry somebody with money as it is to marry somebody poor. It's just as easy to marry someone handsome as it is to marry the guy with "a great personality." All it takes is "I do," and you did. In the same breath, it's just as easy to decide to do something right as it is to do something wrong. Perhaps it doesn't *feel* as easy at the time, but it's as simple as deciding and following through. Choices matter. God ordained marriage in such a way that we're supposed to be choosing whom we're linking ourselves up with for the rest of our lives. That other person is intended to be your partner forever, so choose wisely. Your husband is either going to limit or increase your capacity to grow in God. He is in a position to hold you back or encourage you in many, many areas. When making a decision, think longer-term than merely charisma and cash; think about whether this person is going to encourage you in your relationship with Christ.

ENGAGING HEAVEN

If you're married, pray for your husband. If you're single, pray for your future husband. If you don't plan to get married, pray for friends to link up with who will encourage you in your walk with Christ.

God's Purpose for Your Life

All things were created through Him and for Him.
COLOSSIANS 1:16 NKJV

All of us have a reason to live. God created everything with a beautiful design in mind. He created plants with a purpose, animals with intentionality, and he created *you* with the utmost love and care. He has a specific and important purpose for you to be here. If you're breathing today and your heart is beating, there is a reason you're alive. Do you know what your purpose is? So many people don't. The key to finding your reason for existence is by looking to the one who created you. The number one reason you're on this earth is to know and love God. And when you do that, you'll see more clearly the specifics of what you're here to do. The Lord doesn't want you to worry; he's going to take care of you. If he cares for the plants and the animals, he's certainly going to take great care of you too.

ENGAGING HEAVEN

Do you feel lost in your purpose? Have you asked your Father why he created you the certain way that he did?

Those Who Obey

My beloved brethren, be steadfast, immovable,
always abounding in the work of the Lord,
knowing that your labor is not in vain in the Lord.

1 Corinthians 15:58 NKJV

The Bible says that Jesus "learned obedience by the things which He suffered" (Hebrews 5:8 NKJV). Listen, if Jesus had to learn obedience, how much more so do we have to? We're going to face situations where we're tempted to speak or act in the flesh, and we have to choose instead to operate in the spirit realm. Instead of looking for an easy way out, let's ask, "What is God saying?" "What is he doing?" In truth, God is doing mighty works, and he does them through obedient people. So don't fret about the tests when they come and just stay obedient. It's in the hard times—not the easy—when true obedience is tested and proven. Even if we feel like we might break, we can know that God will rebuild us and that will be a greater testimony to the world of what God can do with a broken person who's willing to say yes.

ENGAGING HEAVEN

Are you willing to obey God, even in the face of suffering?

Hearing versus Doing

If anyone is a hearer of the word and not a doer,
he is like a man observing his natural face in a mirror;
for he observes himself, goes away,
and immediately forgets what kind of man he was.
JAMES 1:23–24 NKJV

When Jesus was preparing to leave the earth, he gave his followers their final instructions: go, preach, baptize, cast out demons, and so forth (Mark 16:15–18). All these commands were action-based. He never mentions consuming as many sermon messages as possible, reading all the books, or listening to a podcast a day. That wasn't the goal. The goal of Christianity isn't to sit comfortably in church. It's to grow within the church and take it to the nations. Christians today take in so much information and do so little with it, and that is why the gospel is not advancing like God intends it to. We have become a generation of hearers only. We are the ultimate consumers. Our ambition should be to foster meaningful relationships and put feet to concrete regarding the things God has asked us to do. We need to be hearers *and* doers. Obedience changes everything.

ENGAGING HEAVEN

When you hear something impactful,
what do you do with it?

As for You

But you, Timothy, have closely followed my example and the truth that I've imparted to you. You have modeled your life after the love and endurance I've demonstrated in my ministry by not giving up. The faith I have, you now have. What I have hungered for in life has now become your longing as well. The patience I have with others, you now demonstrate.

2 Timothy 3:10 TPT

After listing some sobering qualities of the end times in 2 Timothy 3:1–5, Paul commended Timothy's conduct in verse 10. Timothy had carefully followed his doctrine and had demonstrated a life of "purpose, faith, longsuffering, love, [and] perseverance" (NKJV). That's quite a commendable resume. As evil as the world was, Timothy lived counter-culturally. He shone like a light in a dark world. Our world is still dark today, and we must refuse to blend in with its way of living. There's a "but you" moment when you will be identified either with the world or as a daughter of light. What you do in the face of evil is going to define your "but you" clause. You cannot control what happens to you—all manner of unfortunate events happened to Paul—you can only control how you react to it. Learn to live in peace and respond to darkness with light.

ENGAGING HEAVEN

Create a list of the blessings in your life. When you encounter potholes in your path, remind yourself of these blessings.

Distracted Life

The single woman is focused on the things of the Lord so she can be holy both in body and spirit. But a married woman is concerned about the things of the world and how she may please her husband. I am trying to help you...so that you would have undistracted devotion, serving the Lord constantly with an undivided heart.

1 CORINTHIANS 7:34–35 TPT

Paul was explaining to the Corinthian church the dangers of being distracted. Even if they were married, they were expected to live in such devotion to God that it would be as if they were single: single-minded toward the Father. With so much information and entertainment at our fingertips, we are living in the most distracted days ever. Our relationships are suffering. We have replaced feelings with emojis. Pictures aren't the real thing. We are missing moments that matter because all we want to do is capture something. Life is not on Instagram. Life is way better. Children relate love to time. Do you want to love your children? Spend time with them. When you're with them, are you present, or is your mind always somewhere else? Living distracted is hindering our relationships, including our relationship with Jesus. When we break free of distractions, that's when we can truly step into the life God has planned for us. God does not want barriers between us and him.

ENGAGING HEAVEN

What are the areas in your life that you need to remove so you can draw close to God the way he intended you to?

No Reputation

Christ Jesus...made Himself of no reputation,
taking the form of a bondservant,
and coming in the likeness of men.

Philippians 2:5, 7 NKJV

The King of the universe, Jesus, made himself of no reputation. Yet here we are today, so busy trying to maintain something that won't even matter to us beyond this temporary life: our reputations. When we go to heaven, we can't take our likes and our followers with us. All that's going to matter is what God thinks. Who did we impact for the kingdom? Whose life was changed because of how we lived? When someone dies, it doesn't matter to them whether we praise them or curse them because they're dead. They're not trying to maintain their reputations anymore; they're standing before their Creator. Only God can make us great, and there's nothing wrong with greatness when it comes from God, who is the only one qualified to determine greatness. But do you remember whom he said would be great in the kingdom? Matthew 20:26 says, "Whoever desires to become great among you, let him be your servant" (NKJV). Let's live with no reputation of our own and make Jesus famous on this earth.

ENGAGING HEAVEN

If you want a reputation, give up yours. If you want to be great in the kingdom, serve others.

Every Little Thing

I'm writing to encourage you to pray with gratitude to God.
Pray for all men with all forms of prayers
and requests as you intercede with intense passion.

1 TIMOTHY 2:1 TPT

When all Jesus had was one boy's lunch to feed thousands
of hungry people, he looked to his Father in heaven and
thanked him for providing before the food actually multiplied
(Matthew 14:19). When Lazarus died, Jesus first thanked
God for hearing him before he raised his friend from the
dead (John 11:41). If we can thank God in the midst of what
appears to be lack, we will soon realize that we were never
actually lacking anything. The answer we needed was waiting
for us all along; we simply had to look at him to see it. Be
the kind of person who notices God in every little thing. The
minute you're tempted to speak out of your flesh and state
the obvious, state the supernatural instead. Decide that you
will refuse to be a mouthpiece for the enemy. There will be
resurrection power to a generation who will learn to thank
God in the midst of what appears to be lack because they
know that in Christ, they have all they need.

ENGAGING HEAVEN

*What do you lack in life? Do you believe God will provide
for all your needs?*

Idle Talk

O Timothy! Guard what was committed to your trust,
avoiding the profane and idle babblings
and contradictions of what is falsely called knowledge.

1 TIMOTHY 6:20 NKJV

Godless chatter. Idle babblings. Arguments. Gossip. Not to mention all the needless quarrels online. We can't give in to what people falsely call "knowledge," which is just idle talk. We have a higher calling as ambassadors of Christ. We have access to the Word of God, which is the timeless letter of wisdom and true knowledge. As Paul instructed Timothy in 1 Timothy 1:18, we must be ready to "wage the good warfare" and refuse to engage in the meaninglessness of it all. What war are you waging? Do you allow people to dump all their verbal garbage on you? Do you pause at the watercooler at work and partake in the gossip? Do you laugh at the expense of someone else to save your own face? Or have you set up healthy boundaries and drawn a line in the sand? Satan wants to distract us and cause us to lose the power of our words. So, when someone tries to bring out the worst in you online or in person, shut it down. Wage the good war, and Christ will be revealed through you.

ENGAGING HEAVEN

What does it look like to wage war on worthless words?

Guarding Your Deposit

Take heed to yourself and to the doctrine.
Continue in them, for in doing this you will save
both yourself and those who hear you.

1 TIMOTHY 4:16 NKJV

First Timothy 6:20, says "O Timothy! Guard what was committed to your trust, avoiding the profane and idle babblings and contradictions of what is falsely called knowledge." What Paul was saying to Timothy was that he needed to guard the principles that had been instilled in him, the things that shaped his heart, the integrity that God gave him. Fight for those things. Don't surrender any ground in that area because they're hard to come by and easily lost. Our doctrine in this current generation is so intangible. We're so caught up trying to figure out what's right and what's wrong that we're not guarding the deposit that we've been given—the deposit of faith and the knowledge of truth that generations before us passed down. When it comes to faith and the principles of God, they don't change. Jesus paid a huge price to offer them to us. It's our job now to guard what God has given us, not let the world tarnish it, hold the line, and be an example for future generations.

ENGAGING HEAVEN

Is there a biblical principle that you struggle to maintain in your everyday life? How do you plan to hold the line and guard it?

November

Shine Bright

"I am the light of the world.
He who follows Me shall not walk in darkness,
but have the light of life."
JOHN 8:12 NKJV

Every time you see success or breakthrough, there's always something more going on behind the curtain. When you flip a light switch, you see a bulb light up, but the reality is that the bulb doesn't have much power on its own. There's a secret source of power hidden in the walls. There's a grid somewhere in the city. So, although the result is a lit bulb, there are many factors that need to be just right for that light to shine. In the same way, when you see breakthrough, success, or something else powerful, remember that there is more going on than you can see, and the not-so-secret source of the greatest power is Jesus. If you're connected to God and plugged in to his Word, he will put his power in you, and you will most definitely shine bright in this dark world.

ENGAGING HEAVEN

Are you plugged into God's power, or are you trying to shine on your own?

Looking Up

[God] raised us up together,
and made us sit together
in the heavenly places in Christ Jesus.
EPHESIANS 2:6 NKJV

God wants to take your position on this earth and grant you a promotion. You've already been assigned a seat with him, so now he wants you to open your eyes to the position you actually have. Do you want to see God's kingdom come to earth just as it is in heaven? Well, he wants to use you to help accomplish that. Figure out what the Father is doing because it certainly pertains to you. Become obsessed with kingdom life. Become obsessed with Holy Spirit culture. It isn't possible to operate in the kingdom if your mind is set on things here on earth. How can you tell if your mindset is earth-focused or kingdom-focused? Well, how much of your day is spent reacting to this world? Do you give the news more attention than you give the Word of God? No, we can't ignore the world, but the truth is we are each going to reflect the kingdom we're most invested in and aware of.

ENGAGING HEAVEN

Are you stuck in a rut, wondering what your calling is? Have you considered the position you hold in heaven?

Healthy Boundaries

He might present her to Himself a glorious church,
not having spot or wrinkle or any such thing,
but that she should be holy and without blemish.
EPHESIANS 5:27 NKJV

The Lord gives us the responsibility to decide when we
will spend time with him. He gives us the option to choose
healthy boundaries. There is peace in those boundaries.
There's breakthrough in making healthy choices. There's
a better life waiting for those committed to putting him
first, but we each have to decide that for ourselves. If we
want the fruit of an abundant life, we need to set healthy
boundaries. It's important to establish barriers to protect our
kids, our families, our marriages, and our own spiritual health.
Upholding integrity and character is an important step to
guarding what has been entrusted to us. If we're going to
see our families transformed, if we're going to stand for the
things of God in a culture that doesn't respect him, it's going
to require setting boundaries and marking those barriers. The
trumpet is going to sound, and he is coming back again for a
bride without spot or wrinkle.

ENGAGING HEAVEN

*What are some boundaries you have set for yourself
or your family?*

Cruise Control

My brethren, count it all joy when you fall into various trials,
knowing that the testing of your faith produces patience.
But let patience have its perfect work, that you may be
perfect and complete, lacking nothing.

JAMES 1:2–4 NKJV

As a society, we've become addicted to comfort. We want
our marriages to be comfortable, our relationships to be
easy, and our Christianity to be convenient. Essentially, we
want our lives on cruise control. We don't like bumps or trials,
and we run from conflict. Well, comfort can be a blessing
and a curse. See, the beautiful thing about our relationship
with God is there absolutely will be trials and tests. There
have to be because we don't get a testimony without a test.
Unfortunately, our generation is so addicted to comfort that
we never discover the beautiful breakthrough that comes
through endurance and growth. We don't witness miracles
without trials. It's through resistance that we grow and
experience the greatest breakthroughs. If all we're doing is
enjoying our cruise control Christianity, it's the perfect setup
for a crash.

ENGAGING HEAVEN

What truths make you uncomfortable?

Redeem the Time

Walk circumspectly...redeeming the time,
because the days are evil.
EPHESIANS 5:15-16 NKJV

Productivity is suffering today. Work is not being accomplished because people are distracted. They are focused on their own lives. Many people want to be entrepreneurs, but they lack the work ethic. The Bible is very clear that "Slackers will know what it means to be poor, while the hard worker becomes wealthy" (Proverbs 10:4 TPT). It is very hard to be a disciplined, diligent person in the day we live in. If you truly want to grow more in love with the Father and you want to do all the great things God has called you to do, then you need to remove all the obstacles distracting you from pursuing that. Perhaps you used to be a mighty woman of God but over time you settled for a mediocre life. You are a spiritual farmer, and what you reap is what you're going to sow. If you don't like what you're reaping, reconsider what you're sowing. Conviction keeps us burning. Keeping the right priorities matters.

ENGAGING HEAVEN

What are you reaping? What are you sowing?

Monday Isn't the Problem

> May the Lord of peace Himself
> give you peace always in every way.
> The Lord be with you all.
> 2 Thessalonians 3:16 NKJV

God wired all of us differently. There's the part of our day that makes a living, and there's the part of our day that makes a life. If we're dissatisfied with how we're making a living, we will also struggle in the life department. It's important that we don't blame Monday for our lack of peace because that's not where the true problem lies. If there's no peace in our hearts, we need to find out where the brokenness is and stop dreading Mondays. It's important that we love ourselves enough to ask, "What am I doing or not doing that is stealing my joy?" It could be that we need to make more time for the kingdom or for our families. Perhaps it means switching careers to something more fulfilling and learning to live on less. When we look back on our lives, we're going to remember the life we created, not the living wage we earned.

ENGAGING HEAVEN

How do you normally feel Monday morning?

Forgetting Things

However I do have one compelling focus:
I forget all of the past as I fasten my heart
to the future instead.

PHILIPPIANS 3:13 TPT

Fear lives in our past, and faith lives in our future. Jesus even warned, "No one, having put his hand to the plow, and looking back, is fit for the kingdom of God" (Luke 9:62 NKJV). If our lives are structured around fears of the past, it's time to let them go. How you handle today will determine where you go tomorrow. We've all done things in our past that we are ashamed of today. Thank God, they're under the blood. But something people don't often understand is that we need to let go of the good things also. This is so hard to understand because we're all nostalgic, and we cling to our good memories. But if we're caught up in always trying to recreate good memories, how can we make new ones? If we're still living off the rush of past successes, how will we be driven to keep succeeding? How will we ever find anything greater if we're always looking backward?

ENGAGING HEAVEN

You are a miracle worker. You are destined and designed by God to change this world. So, press on!

Don't Neglect

Do not neglect the gift that is in you,
which was given to you by prophecy
with the laying on of the hands of the eldership.
Meditate on these things; give yourself entirely to them,
that your progress may be evident to all.

1 TIMOTHY 4:14–15 NKJV

What does it mean to neglect the gift that is in you? Paul warned Timothy to not do this, so how can we heed his words of caution too? A good place to start is remembering what God has done for you and what he has put in you. Don't neglect these things and, instead, meditate on them. Paul said to give ourselves entirely to them. Entirely to what? Not to speaking idly. Not to trusting in riches. But to reading, to sharing the good news, to studying the teachings of Jesus, and to the other gifts we receive through the Holy Spirit. If you continue in the ways of God, meditating on them and not neglecting them, you will see yourself and your household transformed. Be an example. Whether you realize it or not, your family is watching, others are watching, so be an example. When you become the example Christ wants you to be, God is going to have his way in your life. He is going to make his perfect plan come forth through you. You just need patience.

ENGAGING HEAVEN

What gifts has God given you and put in you?

The Radical Middle

Oh, taste and see that the LORD is good;
Blessed is the man who trusts in Him!
PSALM 34:8 NKJV

The enemy wants to reduce Christianity to a principle. True, it is principles, and we absolutely live by principle, but we also live by presence and by relationship. If we're only living by the letter of the law, then we're missing out on what this life is really about. On the other hand, if we're just living by experience, we're going to be easily picked off. If we're not careful, we can easily become addicted to the feeling of Christianity rather than being in love with the Creator, but that won't last long when trials and temptation come. So, really, we're on a quest for the radical middle. We need to live by principle and understand the Word of God, but we also need the Spirit to fill us with great measure. That's the perfect equation for an abundant life: the experience of the Spirit and the steadfast Word of God. We were created to encounter God. We were never meant to live outside of that encounter.

ENGAGING HEAVEN

Are you leaning too far toward one side or the other? What helps you maintain that radical middle?

High Heat

Because you are neither cold nor hot, but lukewarm,
I am about to spit you from my mouth.
REVELATION 3:16 TPT

There are two ways to read the Bible: with or without the Holy Spirit. When you read the Scriptures, does the fire of God ignite you and cause a burning desire to share it and start seeing souls saved? Or is it a demanding job for you as you just try to earn God's love? It seems we're so scared today to pray aloud or call sin "sin" because we just want to be understanding and tolerant. But that's not how Jesus lived and not how we're expected to live either. It's time to pull away from this current dead system of Christianity. Don't be safe; be extreme! Stand up to the heat. Declare in your heart today that you're going to burn for God. Love people unconditionally and be willing to let the touch of God move through your life. Speak a word in due season and let life flow from you.

ENGAGING HEAVEN

When people look at you, do they know beyond a doubt that you're the kind of woman who believes and stands for everything the Bible says?

Easily Distracted

If then you were raised with Christ,
seek those things which are above,
where Christ is, sitting at the right hand of God.

COLOSSIANS 3:1 NKJV

We live in the most distracted day that's ever been seen. Online life isn't real life. If your life can be deleted by a social media account, you're not living a real life. If your influence is limited to a Facebook post, you don't have true influence. Because if all these social media accounts can be deleted, what eternal value does your life hold? Are you leading people? Is there personal touch in your life? Is there influence? Are you reaching out and sharing your faith? Are you loving on people? Or are you consumed with watching other peoples' lives? A personal touch goes beyond talking on the internet. Social media can be a great tool to share and communicate with others, but it needs to be used in its proper place. If you use it in excess, it will destroy you.

ENGAGING HEAVEN

What personal limits have you put in place to safeguard against getting distracted from your real life by online life?

Cross Fighting

Remind them of these things,
charging them before the Lord not to strive
about words to no profit, to the ruin of the hearers.
2 TIMOTHY 2:14 NKJV

If we're going to talk about the cross, then let's talk about
what happened on Calvary. Let's talk about what the Lord
paid for us. Let's talk about his presence and power at work
in our life. As Christians, equally loved and forgiven by the
Lord, let's not sit around and argue about the details of a
wooden cross. Is this what Christianity has come to? We're
just debating to debate. We've become a culture that would
rather argue about trite differences of interpreting the
Scriptures than receive them, live them, and share them with
others. We will never see the gospel go forth in power and
lives changed if we continue to live in petty ways. Where
there is no power and where there is no presence, people
resort to becoming petty. James 1:22 tells us to "Be doers
of the word, and not hearers only, deceiving yourselves"
(NKJV). What are you doing? You have been given so much
on the cross, so how are you using it?

ENGAGING HEAVEN

*What are you going to do with the power of the resurrection
of the cross? Argue with other Christians or show them love?*

Mind of Christ

Let this mind be in you
which was also in Christ Jesus.
PHILIPPIANS 2:5 NKJV

The Bible says that we have the mind of Christ (1 Corinthians
2:16), yet today, people's minds are all over the place. It
requires a decision to live with peace and joy and to put
on the mind of Christ. If we want joy—real happiness—it is
found in God's presence (Psalm 16:11). That's it. Our minds
cannot find joy or renewal anywhere other than his presence.
It doesn't exist any other place. So today, if you want to see
victory and you want to live your best life, it's going to be in
his presence. If you want to combat a generation that has lost
all meaningful impact in life, you're going to find that missing
meaning in his presence. If you're longing for a renewal of
peace or joy, God has it for you. If you want to hear his voice,
you're going to have to turn down the volume of the world,
enter his presence, and allow joy to be restored in your heart.

ENGAGING HEAVEN

*When was the last time you set aside everything else and
spent uninterrupted time in God's presence?*

Eyes Opened

The eyes of your understanding being enlightened; that you may know what is the hope of His calling, what are the riches of the glory of His inheritance in the saints.

EPHESIANS 1:18 NKJV

The things God has put in front of you—family, job, church, ministry, the poor—all hold valuable opportunity. If you don't perceive it, somebody else will, and they'll receive the value from it. We can become so unhappy in the greatest circumstances. A grateful heart is everything. It's time to look at the people and opportunities God have given you and thank him for them. Take advantage of your circumstances and realize that what you have is what somebody else is praying for. What you have been given, other people see value in. Something or someone else is not going to make you better; the only thing that's going to set you free is when you are thankful for what God gave you. The grass isn't greener on the other side of the fence. It's greener when you water the grass you're standing on. I pray that our eyes would be opened, and we would have more gratefulness and thanksgiving than ever before.

ENGAGING HEAVEN

What relationships, opportunities, and blessings has God given you?

Prayer Life

Be anxious for nothing, but in everything by prayer and supplication, with thanksgiving, let your requests be made known to God; and the peace of God, which surpasses all understanding, will guard your hearts and minds through Christ Jesus.

PHILIPPIANS 4:6–7 NKJV

Prayer is simply talking to God. We can try to puff it up with eloquent words, but in its purest form, it's having a conversation with our Father. The Bible says we don't have because we don't ask (James 4:2), and so many people live without because they don't pray about it; they don't believe the truth that God is generous, caring, and desires to supply for all our needs. God offers us faith and peace, and the biggest hinderance to having peace is not asking for it in prayer. When we don't pray, we don't receive peace. Jesus told us to pray so we wouldn't fall into temptation (Matthew 26:41). Sure, we may overcome the temptation, but why bring unnecessary fighting into our lives? If we're not having one-on-one time with the Father and we're not praying for and receiving his gifts, we're opening ourselves up to fear, anxiety, depression, torment, and so forth. Fear is the opposite of faith, so always remember to pray and establish a prayer life.

ENGAGING HEAVEN

The devil tries to make things bigger than they really are, and the first thing he's going to do is try to distract your prayer life. Protect your prayer life so God can give you a perspective of faith instead of fear.

Feed Growth

Now is the time for us to progress beyond the basic
message of Christ and advance into perfection.
The foundation has already been laid for us to build upon:
turning away from our dead works to embrace faith in God.

HEBREWS 6:1 TPT

Leaders are readers. Leaders challenge themselves to get
out of their comfort zones. What are we doing to challenge
ourselves and get stronger? Why is Christianity one of the
only areas where we tend to always eat only what we like?
What would happen to us physically if all we ate was our
favorite desserts? We wouldn't make it very long. How are
you growing in faith? Who in your life is challenging you in
the areas you're weak in? Are you eating the spiritual food
that's healthy for you and not just consuming your favorite
verses over and over? There is an unhealthy mentality that
many Christians have resorted to that treats church like a
performance. They arrive Sunday morning and, with very
little contribution from themselves, critique the "show." They
forget the message by lunch. They aren't challenged to grow,
and they're comfortable in their seats. It takes discipline to
get out of our seats, accepting the challenge to embrace the
uncomfortable, but that's how we make a difference. That's
how we grow.

ENGAGING HEAVEN

*How are you challenging yourself in your spiritual journey
this week?*

At the Break of Dawn

A new commandment I write to you,
which thing is true in Him and in you,
because the darkness is passing away,
and the true light is already shining.

1 JOHN 2:8 NKJV

Certain principles in the Word of God never end. Darkness is temporary, but the true light of Christ is everlasting. Darkness cannot stand light because light always wins. If you bring a single light into a dark room, the darkness cannot extinguish it. And no matter what darkness you're facing today, Christ's light is going to win. Darkness hides what light exposes. Darkness is suffocating and can make you feel like there's no hope, but the dawn of a new day is over your life. The presence and power of Jesus is with you. The Bible says, "We are hard-pressed on every side, yet not crushed; we are perplexed, but not in despair; persecuted, but not forsaken; struck down, but not destroyed" (2 Corinthians 4:8–9 NKJV). Darkness cannot destroy you because it is temporary, and you are eternally secure in Christ. It's a new day, so go and reflect light everywhere you go in Jesus' name.

ENGAGING HEAVEN

How can you find hope in a seemingly hopeless situation?

One Kingdom

I exhort first of all that supplications, prayers,
intercessions, and giving of thanks be made for all men,
for kings and all who are in authority,
that we may lead a quiet and peaceable life
in all godliness and reverence.

1 TIMOTHY 2:1-2 NKJV

God raises and demotes authority, and it is on us to respect those in authority and to pray for them, no matter who they are. Our number one desire in life should be to bring people to Jesus because he is the authority above every other authority. No political party, president, or pastor is worthy of our complete allegiance, but they are worthy of our respect and prayers because they were placed in our lives by God. They will answer for their decisions before God, but that is not for us to judge. Our job is to pray for them. If we want a peaceful and godly life, let's do our job, pray for our authority, and leave the judging up to God. He is, after all, the only perfect judge *and* the ultimate authority.

ENGAGING HEAVEN

Which authority figures will you pray for today?

God Is Moving

I thank my God...being confident of this very thing,
that He who has begun a good work in you
will complete it until the day of Jesus Christ.
PHILIPPIANS 1:3, 6 NKJV

At times, the Lord will, through a testing period, make adjustments for you to succeed. Remember when you're going through unique circumstances that God is moving. He shows you grace and love by preparing you. Greatness can come from this. There are times of intense pressure in life, when it feels like leaks are being exposed, but that is because he is protecting you, patching you up, and getting things fixed. When you come out of this season, you're going to be stronger and better than ever. This is not just for some far-off crusade down the road, but it's also for today. It's so you can be a great wife, a great mother, and learn to have peace in your everyday life, with your job, with your family *today*. God has given you grace and peace and mercy and breakthrough because he is setting you up for victory. He is moving.

ENGAGING HEAVEN

*Do you see God moving in your life? Even when you don't
see movement, do you trust that he's there?*

Disney Dreams

I can do all things
through Christ who strengthens me.
PHILIPPIANS 4:13 NKJV

Isn't Philippians 4:13 a great verse? But did you realize Paul was in prison when he penned it? As great as this verse is, we cannot overlook the one preceding it: "I know how to be abased, and I know how to abound. Everywhere and in all things I have learned both to be full and to be hungry, both to abound and to suffer need" (v. 12 NKJV). See, Paul knew that God promised to give him strength. He was not promised an easy life. The key is contentment in Christ. If you think that landing a perfect job is going to bring you contentment, you're wrong. If you think that finally finding your Prince Charming is the missing piece to your happiness, you're going to be disappointed. Don't fall for these broken Disney dreams because it doesn't matter if you're in the Magic Kingdom or in prison; your joy and contentment and strength come only from the Lord. Any other promise is a lie from the enemy.

ENGAGING HEAVEN

How can you practically keep the same faith, confidence, and contentment both when life is going well and when it's going poorly?

Birthing Promise

"A woman giving birth experiences
intense labor pains in delivering her baby,
yet after the child is born
she quickly forgets what she went through
because of the overwhelming joy of knowing
that a new baby has been born into the world."
JOHN 16:21 TPT

Birthing children hurts. With or without pain killers, it hurts. There are contractions that precede birth. When people face trials and testing in life, they ask, "What is all this pain? What is happening? Why do I have to feel this way?" Well, those are contractions. God wants to birth something great through you, but it is often preceded by pain. And it will probably be messy, as life often is. Birth is messy and birthing hurts. There is pain in progress, but it brings forth life. It brings forth a miracle. Three women in the Bible gave birth in the face of impossibility: Sarah, Elizabeth, and Mary. If your life feels impossible right now, hang on. God may be preparing you to birth in circumstances that may seem crazy but will bring great glory to him. Dream with God. Prepare your heart for whatever it is he wants to bring forth from you. It's time to lock in on the plan God has for you. All the pain you're feeling is just the birthing season.

ENGAGING HEAVEN

Read the stories of Sarah (Genesis 18:1–16, 21:1–7), Elizabeth, and Mary (Luke 1:5–80, 2:1–20). What can you learn from these women?

Expressing Thankfulness

"Praise the LORD, call upon His name;
Declare His deeds among the peoples,
Make mention that His name is exalted."

ISAIAH 12:4 NKJV

Thanksgiving is the entryway of worship. We enter his gates by way of thanksgiving. Thanksgiving is for us. Thanksgiving is our response to the acts of God. It's our recognition of what he's done. See, it's not enough to simply have a thankful heart because we're expected to open our mouths and declare it. Thanksgiving is active; it's acknowledging the good things God has done. The Bible says *give* thanks to God (1 Thessalonians 5:18). The Father's desire is that we express thanksgiving. If you feel thankful for all your husband does or all your parents do or for your friends, they're not going to feel appreciated unless you tell them. "Thank you for going to work every day for our family." "Thank you for being there when I needed you." An interesting thing happens when we express thanksgiving: we start to live more thankfully. Often our actions follow our words, so by confessing our gratitude to God, our body and our actions also begin to realign.

ENGAGING HEAVEN

What are you thankful for today? Tell God, then tell your other loved ones.

Hallelujah Anyhow!

Enter into His gates with thanksgiving,
And into His courts with praise.
Be thankful to Him, and bless His name.
PSALM 100:4 NKJV

We enter his gates with thanksgiving, and then we go into his courts with praise. That's because thankfulness precedes praise, and praise is where battles are won. Praise is a weapon that few people use. Praise will win every battle. It is the access point to the deeper realms of God. Praise is often misunderstood because it is less of a feeling and more of an offering. Throughout the Bible praise is often described as a sacrifice (see Jeremiah 33:11 and Hebrews 13:15, for example). When we go through trials, the last thing we feel like doing is praising, but it will transform us when we give it as a sacrifice. Praise is not about us feeling good. Many times, when we're praising, we're doing it out of just knowing who he is, how good he is, that he's worthy of it. In thanksgiving, we respond to God. In praise, we acknowledge who he is.

ENGAGING HEAVEN

If you don't have any money, hallelujah anyhow. If you're sick in bed, hallelujah anyhow. Regardless of how you feel, hallelujah anyhow.

Divine Delay

Jesus replied,
"You don't understand yet the meaning of what I'm doing,
but soon it will be clear to you."
JOHN 13:7 TPT

There are some moments in life when God chooses to cover things and let them germinate. There are other moments when he chooses to act. How we use those times of germination will determine how ready we are to act when the time comes. We have to allow him his due process because he tarries for our benefit. Obviously, God is ready any time, but we have limits. Times of waiting, hoping, and germinating are important so we can focus our hearts and minds on God's goodness and remember where our hope and our strength come from. Discouragement can set in easily, even to the point where our impatience makes our hearts feel sick. But if we have faith to hold on, those moments when God is ready to move and act are like life that springs up within us. We'll be ready.

ENGAGING HEAVEN

What happens when God doesn't meet our timeline?

Keep the Name

"If I'm not doing the beautiful works that my Father sent me to do, then don't believe me. But if you see me doing the beautiful works of God upon the earth, then you should at least believe the evidence of the miracles."

JOHN 10:37–38 TPT

The prophets foretold about Jesus. Creation itself groaned for his reign. All throughout heaven and earth, angels declared his coming. Now, here he was, standing in the midst of the Pharisees and people throwing accusations at him. His response was incredible. "Don't even believe in me," he offered, "but at least believe in the evidence of my miracles." Jesus was healing the sick, raising the dead, casting out demons, and feeding multitudes of people. There was no denying that he had the power of God. There was no denying the evidence. Most of the church today views miracles as optional, not essential. Yet when Jesus was praying, he declared, "And the glory which You gave Me I have given them" (John 17:22 NKJV). We are on this earth to prove the love and existence of Christ as our King. But why would anyone believe in a church that preaches but doesn't perform? No, the Christian life was not meant to be lived without the miraculous power of God.

ENGAGING HEAVEN

Start believing in miracles again. Start praying for your family. We are Spirit-filled believers and miracle workers. We are called to reign in life, and anything less is a compromise.

All In

"I am the way, the truth, and the life.
No one comes to the Father except through Me."
JOHN 14:6 NKJV

The question we all need to ask is, "Who is Jesus Christ to me?" The Bible is clear that there is no other way to heaven but through Jesus Christ, and this is nonnegotiable. But it's not enough to simply *know* who Jesus is; we also need to encounter him. When we encounter Jesus, the God of all glory and all power, we are forever changed. We can never be the same again. Forget everything you've been told and any preconceived notion you have. When you encounter Jesus through relationship, he ignites a fire in you that burns and consumes every area of your life. Do you know him personally, intimately? Because that fire is for every believer. We are called to walk as heavenly people, covered in his glory and power. We were never meant to live without encounter. Don't become okay with living a low-level life. Encounter Jesus and experience that transforming fire.

ENGAGING HEAVEN

Are you all in? Have you given everything to Jesus? Have you encountered him?

Release It

"Lazarus is dead.
And I am glad for your sakes that I was not there,
that you may believe.
Nevertheless let us go to him."
JOHN 11:14–15 NKJV

The loved ones of Lazarus thought Jesus was coming, so when he was delayed, they became upset. When Jesus finally did come, Mary and some of the Jews who accompanied her cried, saying, "Lord, if You had been here, my brother would not have died" (v. 32 NKJV). Little did they know what Jesus had planned, that Lazarus would rise from the dead and that all of this was for the glory of God. If we're going to walk in faith, there are things we have to release to God. God cannot hold on to something if we're holding on to it. Lazarus was buried. They had to let him go for Jesus to work his wonders. And when Jesus died, they buried him and rolled the stone in front. Each of us will face times in life when we need to bury something we love and roll a stone in front of it. Give it to God. Release it. Then step back and watch him work.

ENGAGING HEAVEN

What do you need to release into God's hands? Your kids? Your dreams? This doesn't mean be negligent...only give God control and have faith.

Darkest Places

"You shall receive power when the Holy Spirit has come upon
you; and you shall be witnesses to Me in Jerusalem,
and in all Judea and Samaria, and to the end of the earth."
Acts 1:8 NKJV

Eyes are being opened in the darkest places of the earth.
We don't have to go overseas to share the good news of the
gospel; we just need to open our eyes right where we are.
There is a harvest field all around us. It's time we allow the
presence of the Holy Spirit to transform our perspectives
because God wants to use us to touch and impact the
darkest places on earth. This is why we're alive right now.
We're here to see the sick healed, the lost found, and the
chains broken off. But we are not going to release dead-
raising power without a connection from God. In order to
have purpose in our lives, we need to connect the power
and presence of God to the problems we see around us. As
Christ's witnesses on earth, we exist so that, through our
testimony, people will recognize that Jesus is real and that he
loves them.

ENGAGING HEAVEN

*What are you dreaming of and aiming for? That will define
the level of breakthrough you expect to experience
in your life.*

No Other Mind

Do not be conformed to this world,
but be transformed by the renewing of your mind,
that you may prove what is that good
and acceptable and perfect will of God.

ROMANS 12:2 NKJV

Your brain has grooves in it, which are actually paths created by thoughts. The good news is you can change your thoughts and change your life. Most of life's battles take place in our minds because our thoughts dictate our decisions. Your mind is like a parking lot, and you have to decide that you're not going to lease any space to anything other than what heaven has for you. Give the devil an eviction notice, and don't allow him a parking spot. This is how you will see transformation. It is by a renewed mind that a life is transformed and the will of God is proven. So, don't conform to a dead church world. Don't conform to mediocre Christianity. Don't conform to worldly thoughts that carve dangerous grooves in your mind. Be transformed by a renewed mind and a heart that burns for God and God alone.

ENGAGING HEAVEN

Does God's will get you excited and set your heart on fire?

Cultivating Promise

"Abide in Me, and I in you.
As the branch cannot bear fruit of itself,
unless it abides in the vine,
neither can you, unless you abide in Me."

JOHN 15:4 NKJV

When you give birth, it's behind closed doors with only a few important people present. It's private and intimate. But once you have given birth, that's when the celebration begins, and everyone wants to see the baby. The process is similar to the cycle of heavenly promise. You are pregnant with purpose, and your heart is the womb of promise. Every word God has spoken over you contains power, but you conceive it privately. Not everything that goes on in your life is fodder for the internet; there's something special about pondering God's words in your heart. Allow God to cultivate it and grow it within you through intimacy and abiding with him. In time, the destiny he has produced in you, the dreams and desires he has been growing and nurturing in your heart, will come forth. The time for delivery will come. When what you have been carrying in your heart is ready to be born, it will be beautiful and cause for celebration.

ENGAGING HEAVEN

*Are you nurturing and caring for the dreams and promises
God has placed within you?*

December

Revelation of Faith

Martha said to Jesus, "Lord, if You had been here,
my brother would not have died.
But even now I know that whatever You ask of God,
God will give You."

JOHN 11:21-22 NKJV

When Jesus finally showed up to aid the sick Lazarus, his friend had already been dead and buried for four days. As tragic as it was, Martha was not without hope. See, she knew who Jesus was. She had a revelation of faith that even death had no authority over the authority of her Lord. That's revelation! Revelation does not regard how we feel over the facts of who God is and what his Word says. Even in the face of death, Martha still believed. It takes radical faith to roll the stone away. Whatever it is you are believing for, even now, believe that his hand is upon you. He knows exactly what you need. That's revelation. The centurion with the sick servant revealed his faith and confidence in who Jesus was when he requested, "Say the word, and my servant will be healed" (Luke 7:7 NKJV). When Jesus heard that, he declared, "I have not found such great faith, not even in Israel!" (Luke 7:9 NKJV).

ENGAGING HEAVEN

What is the revelation you need to declare today?

Faith on Vacation

"These things I have spoken to you,
that in Me you may have peace.
In the world you will have tribulation;
but be of good cheer, I have overcome the world."
JOHN 16:33 NKJV

Faith doesn't go on vacation. You can't spend your life sitting poolside, sipping beverages, and think that you're going to be okay. The enemy is up twenty-four hours a day, and so are the angels. This is a spiritual war, friends. We've come to believe that if something makes us uncomfortable, it must be bad. Instead of embracing the different and the difficult, we surround ourselves with people and things that don't offend us, carefully controlling the narrative we want to listen to and live by. But the goal of Christianity isn't to slide through life with as few blows as possible. It's time to get on the offensive and start declaring the Scriptures, believing God at his Word. You don't need to rock the boat; the boat is already rocking. It's time to walk on water. Yes, you can have perfect peace and perfect joy, but life will have turbulence. God is going to equip you to go through whatever you are facing today because you are an overcomer.

ENGAGING HEAVEN

Do you feel the boat rocking? What are you doing about it?

I Want

"Whatever you ask in My name,
that I will do, that the Father may be glorified in the Son.
If you ask anything in My name, I will do it."
JOHN 14:13–14 NKJV

When we're in the midst of prayer, things change, mindsets change, who we are changes. God will bring forth the *true* desires of our hearts, the desires he placed there and molded us for. These desires are often buried beneath all the world's worries, but prayer clears the clouds. We each have a battle waging inside of us between who the world has told us to be and who God says that we are. There can't be two lords of our life, so we decide whom to serve by whom we listen to. When we pray, we make the conscious decision to listen to our true Lord and drown out the misleading voice of the enemy. In doing so, our desires change. What we want changes. We are transformed. Now, transformation doesn't happen through one prayer because we are inundated daily with the enemy's propaganda, but through daily spending time with the Lord, praying, and listening, we become who we were meant to be.

ENGAGING HEAVEN

What do you desire?

A Breakthrough Life

"If you abide in Me, and My words abide in you,
you will ask what you desire, and it shall be done for you."
JOHN 15:7 NKJV

So often, we reduce the things of God to a method. But
that is not how the Lord operates. He is not interested in
us just being obedient servants. Rather, he wants loving
and invested children. We need to get our eyes off our
methods and start spending time with our Father. If we want
a breakthrough life, it begins with spending time with God.
If we want our children raised in a godly way, it starts with
spending time with the Lord. Every little breakthrough every
day begins when we pray and believe God is going to use us
in powerful ways. It doesn't matter if you're a mom cooking
breakfast in the morning and your children are your number
one ministry or if your workplace is your mission field;
breakthrough comes through a lifestyle of relationship with
God. When we fast, it's not for a one-time miracle. It's for a
lifestyle that welcomes miracles. We don't live for isolated
incidents but for a relationship with our Father.

ENGAGING HEAVEN

*Read Mark 9:14–29. Was Jesus talking about prayer and
fasting for an isolated incident or as a lifestyle?*

Flowing River

"He who believes in Me, as the Scripture has said,
out of his heart will flow rivers of living water."
JOHN 7:38 NKJV

Only through Christ can a drink become a river, which is a
perfect picture of the kingdom. Only in the kingdom can a
cup become an ocean. The river of almighty God flows within
us when we surrender our lives to him. It is a mighty, rushing
river filled with healing, hope, power, and love. If we want to
see life through God's point of view, then in everything we
should ask God, *What would your kingdom coming to earth as
it is in heaven look like in this situation?* Imagine living every
day in our job, our homes, our schools, with the perspective
of heaven. We could be conduits of heaven, agents of
the kingdom. We could become true carriers of hope in a
desperate world. You don't even understand the world's
negative view anymore. The regular view of earth is dim.

ENGAGING HEAVEN

Read John 7:37–39. What was Jesus talking about?

Be Fruitful, Not Busy

"You didn't choose me,
but I've chosen and commissioned you
to go into the world to bear fruit."
JOHN 15:16 TPT

God never called us to be busy. He called us to bear fruit. Too much pointless activity isn't going to bear fruit. Instead, it's only going to stress us out. We can become very busy doing things that seem important, but we're really accomplishing nothing. It's ineffective and distracting. We need to do some pruning in our lives. We need to cut off the branches that are getting in the way of bearing lasting fruit. What impact do you want to make on this earth? That answer isn't going to be, "I want to go to a university" or "I want to make a lot of money." That answer is going to be, "I want to feed the homeless," "I want to be a missionary," "I want to pray for people," "I want to share my faith," "I want to help those in need," "I want to visit nursing homes," "I want to rescue children from the sex trade." Whatever it is, don't let anything or anyone distract you with busyness.

ENGAGING HEAVEN

What is it God has called you to do? Are there any pointless activities or harmful relationships that are interfering with your calling?

Greater Delay, Greater Glory

"This sickness is not unto death,
but for the glory of God,
that the Son of God may be glorified through it."
JOHN 11:4 NKJV

Lazarus was dead. His loved ones were so frustrated that Jesus waited until *four days* after he had died to come. Why four days? Well, the Jews believed that when someone died, their spirit would still dance around the body and could come back anytime within three days. But the fourth day, it was irrevocable. That person was undeniably gone. Jesus wasn't only interested in healing a sickness. Instead, he had far greater things in mind. He intended to conquer death itself for the glory of God, in a way that no man could receive the credit. We all long to see the glory of God but are so often uncomfortable with his timeline. We don't know how or when God will show up...only that he will. We only have to believe. It's so simple but so difficult. So today, what delayed promises are in the forefront of your mind? What four-day stenches are following you around? What are some victories you thought you would have experienced by now? Jesus is going to come through on all of it. If he is delaying, it is for greater glory.

ENGAGING HEAVEN

What promises are you waiting for?

All Scripture

All Scripture is given by inspiration of God,
and is profitable for doctrine, for reproof,
for correction, for instruction in righteousness.
2 Timothy 3:16 NKJV

What does "all Scripture" mean? It means we don't get to cut out what we don't want to hear. That means we believe in giving, in prayer, and in everything the Bible says. All the Scripture has been given to us, and if we pick and choose what we want to listen to, we're going to get picked off. Having a balanced diet is important. If we only ate ice cream and chocolate, we would be very sick. Having a balanced spiritual diet is even more important. If we only listen to the verses that "taste" good and not the ones that correct or rebuke us, we're going to end up very, very sick. We need the Bible's vegetables as well. It's easy to want to only use our strengths, but *all* Scripture has been given to us. We need to challenge ourselves to embrace the areas that don't come as naturally. That's how we'll stay healthy and balanced in our lives.

ENGAGING HEAVEN

Do you love to worship? Serve? Tithe? Pray? That's great. Challenge yourself this week to embrace some of the things you don't like as much because they're necessary too.

Stand Firm

Take up the whole armor of God,
that you may be able to withstand in the evil day,
and having done all, to stand.
EPHESIANS 6:13 NKJV

The message we preach in the way we conduct ourselves
and the choices we make is important. The message we
live is essential to the fruit we bear and where we'll be long
term. Our response to trials, to pressure, and to warfare will
reveal where we are with God. Whom do we run to? After
we've done everything we know to do, what's our next move?
Are we tripping, or are we kneeling? Are we quitting, or
are we pressing on? Are we retreating from what we know
God wants us to do, or are we willing to follow him into the
unknown? Breakthrough is on the other side of standing
firm. We need to stand our ground, and when we don't know
which way to go, we must continue to stand firm. That is the
secret to an abundant life. When we're under the pressure
of lies, what truth can we stand on? Jesus heals. He saves.
he delivers. He is our Prince of Peace. He is our provider. We
need to know his Word.

ENGAGING HEAVEN

*Read Ephesians 6:10–20. What does it mean to "put on the
whole armor of God" practically in day-to-day living?*

Love Test

May the Lord increase your love until it overflows
toward one another and for all people,
just as our love overflows toward you.

1 Thessalonians 3:12 TPT

Are we increasing and abounding in love? Love is the greatest thing. We need more love in the world. We need to understand what it is to love one another. Let's make a choice to look at life differently, through kingdom glasses, and see people the way God sees them. It's either that or walk around critically and judge others, but if we chose the latter, we would also incur criticism and judgment (Matthew 7:1-2). It's better that we believe the best, love regardless, and leave the judging up to God, who is the only One qualified to correctly make a verdict. Instead of looking for dirt on your friends, start interceding for them and believe for breakthrough in their life. Jesus said we will be known by our love (John 13:35). If nobody knew you were saved and you had never vocally shared the gospel, would they know you were a disciple of Christ because of the way you love others? Or do you just look like the rest of the world?

ENGAGING HEAVEN

What tests are you facing today? Are you learning to love?

Dreaming Big

Now to Him who is able to do exceedingly abundantly above all that we ask or think, according to the power that works in us.

EPHESIANS 3:20 NKJV

Thoughts are like currency, and everybody has a budget. It's important to budget and manage our thoughts because we can't afford to keep wasting our thoughts on things that don't matter. Focus is essential. If we're constantly entertaining negative thoughts, we'll never be able to dream. Proverbs 23:7 tells us that we become what we think in our heart. The power of positive and negative thinking is that we're going to get what we focus on more. No matter what it is we're talking about. The people who focus on their dreams live and breathe what God has put inside them. They get wide-eyed about what the Spirit is bringing to fruition, they fight, work, grow, and don't give up. Today, perhaps, is time to start a new project, break out of the normal cycle, and dream big. It's not going to come easy, which is why focus is so important. Don't let a ceiling stop you. Allow God's dream to sink into your heart and keep your thought life positive.

ENGAGING HEAVEN

What do you want to see happen in your life in the next ten to twenty years?

Give Thanks

In everything give thanks;
for this is the will of God in Christ Jesus for you.
1 THESSALONIANS 5:18 NKJV

The Bible doesn't say to give thanks when times are good or when you get what you want. It says "In everything." We're supposed to give thanks in every situation because, let's be honest, we always have a lot to give God thanks for. When we become distracted by our flesh and the cares of this world, it's easy to get "in our heads" and listen to other influences before we turn to God's Word. The best way for us to recognize what we have and how much there is to be thankful for, is to listen to God's voice and read God's Word first. Let's pray: *Father, we thank you for health even when we don't feel healthy. We thank you for joy even when we don't feel joyful. We thank you for peace because it's a gift. We thank you for our children, our grandchildren, our coworkers, and our friends. We thank you most of all for you.*

ENGAGING HEAVEN

Make a list of the things that God has done for you that you can be thankful for.

Confidence

Faith is the substance of things hoped for,
the evidence of things not seen.
HEBREWS 11:1 NKJV

Faith is assurance. Another word for assurance is *confidence*.
Faith is confidence. As Christians, we walk by faith, not by
what our eyes tell us (2 Corinthians 5:7). If you're living
by what you see, that's not faith. If you're living by what's
going on around you and you're moved by every little thing
the culture tells you, that's not faith. We need to live by the
assurance of our faith, by the confidence we have in God.
Forget what the news is telling you; what does the Word of
God say? The Word of God is your title deed; it's your book
of promises. It is the truest source of information to help
you make life decisions. Faith is a practical expression of the
confidence that you have in God and in his Word.

ENGAGING HEAVEN

*When you hear news that affects you, where do you turn
first? Do you have go-to Scripture verses in hard times?*

It Has Been Released

It is appointed for men to die once,
but after this the judgment.
HEBREWS 9:27 NKJV

It really isn't how you start; it's how you finish. Learn to finish strong. Learn to redeem the time. At the end of our time here on earth, the only thing that remains is what you did for the Lord and what was born of the Spirit. Make sure you're maximizing the opportunities you've been given. Faith is a muscle, and if you don't exercise that muscle, it's never going to strengthen. It's time to get back in the faith gym by digging into your Bible, praying, spending time with the Lord, and saying no to the things of this earth. So many people put their faith in wood, hay, and stubble, but we live within the realms of faith, which is exactly what God wants for us. And as we do, we will see true breakthrough along the way because we are a people of faith. Thank the Lord now in advance—in faith—that he has released his breakthrough to you.

ENGAGING HEAVEN

*What steps are you taking to actively work out
your faith muscle?*

In the Dark

Have no fellowship
with the unfruitful works of darkness,
but rather expose them.
EPHESIANS 5:11 NKJV

The devil dwells in the dark. If we're not calling things out and bringing them to light, the devil will whisper lies about our health, our relationships, our children. We cannot live in the dark because that's where the devil begins to stir stuff in our heads. Let God move. Give him your heart. Give him your life. Instead of overthinking things, call somebody trustworthy and wise so you can clear your head and bring things to light. If you're looking for a sign, the devil is going to give you every sign you want because he is the master of trickery, and he doesn't play fair. Hold fast to what you know is truth—God's truth. Be honest, be open, and if there is something bothering you, let God speak to it.

ENGAGING HEAVEN

Is there anything you're keeping in the dark because, possibly, you're too embarrassed or scared to talk about it? Find someone you trust to offer godly wisdom and be open with her about the help you need.

Declarations

You are a chosen generation, a royal priesthood,
a holy nation, His own special people,
that you may proclaim the praises of Him
who called you out of darkness into His marvelous light.

1 PETER 2:9 NKJV

We're called to be witnesses, but we can't witness for something we haven't witnessed. Some of us need a fresh encounter. We have the Holy Spirit inside of us, and now it's time to tap into that and understand. Do we realize the Word of God is our anchor? Do we understand that our confession has to be grounded in that Word? Second Corinthians 4:13 says, "I believed and therefore I spoke" (NKJV). Whatever it is we're lacking, there's a Scripture passage for it. Are we declaring peace? Are you believing God? Speaking death will curse us. Our words are seeds of power that can be sown for good or for bad—for life or for death. Words are the seeds that go forth into the world and cause a supernatural harvest to occur. We can't sow discord and expect to reap peace.

ENGAGING HEAVEN

When you wake up every morning, declare God's goodness over your life and over your family. Start your day by confessing the Word of God. That will set the trajectory of the rest of your day.

Money and Purpose

The love of money is a root of all kinds of evil, for which some have strayed from the faith in their greediness, and pierced themselves through with many sorrows.

1 Timothy 6:10 NKJV

We are so busy making a living that we fail to make a life. Everything becomes about the bottom dollar, and we lose our focus. There's something freeing about living more simply, about stripping away the excess. There are homeless people who have more peace than some people who live in mansions, so it's not about what we own but the condition of our hearts and what we believe is going to give us a fulfilled life. Fulfillment only comes when we find our purpose and discover what we love to do. Money is needed. We work hard for it, but it's just a tool. Money is not the problem, nor is it the solution. What we do with our money—as well as our time, talents, and other resources—matters far more. In the quest to climb the corporate ladder or in the quicksand trap of accumulating things, many people lose themselves. It's time we get our faith and passion back and do what we were called to do.

ENGAGING HEAVEN

Think about how to create a space to do what you love to do and what you are called to do. What does that look like?

Handling Life

You therefore must endure hardship
as a good soldier of Jesus Christ.
2 TIMOTHY 2:3 NKJV

The Bible is very clear that we're just passing through because we have a greater purpose on the other side, and that's eternity with Jesus. We are here to do God's will, to reconcile people back to him, and to see this world touched by God. When did regular life started becoming overwhelming? Not to belittle problems people are facing, but we can't see those problems as larger than they really are. Sometimes it's not an onslaught from hell. It's just a broken dishwasher. We live in a fallen world, and trials are going to come. Jesus promised offenses and persecutions and trials would come (John 16:33). James says, rejoice when you face trials of many kinds (James 1:2). Tolerance and longsuffering are in short supply, but we have to learn to overcome this life. We have to learn to walk in victory through daily obstacles and disappointments. Every day, we face challenges and difficulties, but that is why we're called to rejoice. We don't get a testimony without a test.

ENGAGING HEAVEN

What difficulties are you facing today? Ask God to give you an eternal perspective on every problem.

Be Doers

Be doers of the word,
and not hearers only,
deceiving yourselves.

JAMES 1:22 NKJV

Unfortunately, a lot of people hear the Word, but they don't obey it. The Father may reveal something in their life that isn't right, but they continue in their same old patterns of destruction. We can't cheer on somebody else's rebuke and not receive correction ourselves. It's important that we also search our own hearts and say yes to God's loving adjustments. There are amazing people who have the potential to change the world, but they disqualify themselves because they choose not to walk in the full counsel of God. You may be anointed, called by God, filled with power, but potential alone isn't enough. Your response to the gospel is what matters.

ENGAGING HEAVEN

Do you really want the full counsel of God today? Are you open to what the Father has to say to you, or are you just going to continue to live blindly?

Love the Church

Let the peace of God rule in your hearts,
to which also you were called in one body;
and be thankful.

COLOSSIANS 3:15 NKJV

If we just sat in our houses feeling bitter toward the church and toward all the people who wronged us, we would accomplish nothing in life. Criticizing the message every Sunday morning and getting upset because people hurt our feelings does nothing but squelch our potential and breed contempt. In short, we have to get over it. Not because the church is perfect but because our focus is supposed to be on God. If God still loves the church and still loves broken, imperfect Christians, then that's our commission as well. When our hearts are grateful for God's grace instead of critical of other people's failings, we won't worry or get offended nearly as much. We'll have no time. We're too busy being flooded with positive thoughts like love, joy, peace, and forgiveness.

ENGAGING HEAVEN

What does God have to say about his love for the church?

Jesus Doesn't Change

Jesus Christ is the same
yesterday, today, and forever.
HEBREWS 13:8 NKJV

When we live in a reactionary culture, most of the decisions we make in life are a reaction to something that has happened to us. But because we live in this reactionary culture, we never feel like we're making progress because we're so busy, caught up in arms over things that simply don't matter. It's time for our society to make Jesus our Rock again. It's time for us to get our eyes off the value of the dollar. Money comes and goes; even its value rises and falls. Since Jesus Christ is the same today as he was yesterday and will be tomorrow, wouldn't it be wiser to stay close to him? If you want to live a stable life, free of worry and fear of the future, free from stress over the latest headlines, cling to the one who doesn't change.

ENGAGING HEAVEN

Do recent news and worldly worries tend to shake your confidence?

Christmas Tree Comparison

They compare themselves to one another
and make up their own standards to measure themselves by,
and then they judge themselves by their own standards.
What self-delusion!

2 CORINTHIANS 10:12 TPT

Around this time of year, everybody starts sending Christmas cards, setting up trees, hanging lights, and enjoying traditions. If we're not careful, it starts to become like a big contest to see who's celebrating the best. Everything becomes about comparison. Other people may not necessarily be trying to make you feel bad, but the devil certainly is. He's going to whisper that your life isn't that great, that you're not doing enough, or that you don't have enough. But it's all a big lie. We don't have to compare ourselves to anyone else. Just enjoy someone else's Christmas tree. Celebrate other people's victories without feeling like a failure yourself. We're all growing and learning, taking step by step down our own path with the Lord. The enemy wants you to look at other people and compare yourself with them, but God just wants you to look at him and let him do what he wants in you.

ENGAGING HEAVEN

What will it take for you to cheer on other people
in their victory?

Overshadow

The angel answered and said to her,
"The Holy Spirit will come upon you,
and the power of the Highest will overshadow you."
LUKE 1:35 NKJV

When the Bible says "overshadow," it means Mary could know that the Lord was going to cover her with his protection and love no matter what came her way. It was the overshadowing of God. The Lord was reassuring Mary that she didn't need to worry about the social fallout of becoming pregnant as a virgin outside of marriage because he was going to cause his glory to surround her and overshadow everything else. She was free and safe to birth what he had called her to birth. Hearing this, Mary surrendered. Without a doubt, she was aware of all the problems she was about to encounter because of this decision, but if God was calling her to it and promised to carry her through it, she would faithfully obey. See, God is looking for worshipers: people who will worship him in spirit and in truth (John 4:24).

ENGAGING HEAVEN

Worshiping in spirit and in truth means that your spirit worships God because he is truth. It means you are faithful even when you don't feel like it.

Glory to God

"Glory to God in the highest,
And on earth peace, goodwill toward men!"
Luke 2:14 NKJV

Christmas is about Jesus. I don't care what day he was born; celebrate his birthday. Fall in love with the Savior. The wise men came to worship. The wise men responded to the birth of the Savior by walking for two years to give him gifts. When the Bible says, "Glory to God in the highest, peace on this earth and goodwill toward men," that word *peace* means "health." Health on earth, sound mind on earth, well-being on earth, prosperity on earth. "Glory to God in the highest *and on earth.*" Wherever you are does not matter. We're not just on earth to pass time until heaven. This time matters too. Settle it within your heart that you will live for God right here and now. Wherever you are, declare peace and goodwill today on earth.

ENGAGING HEAVEN

What purposes do you think God has for you right now where you are, in the current season you're in?

Peace Is a Person

His name will be called Wonderful, Counselor,
Mighty God, Everlasting Father, Prince of Peace.
ISAIAH 9:6 NKJV

God has not established a relationship with us so we would
spend all our time and effort struggling trying to please every
other relationship in our lives and becoming overwhelmed
by them. That is not God's desire for us. What God desires
is an alignment issue because our families, our friends, and
our jobs are not above God. If God is first, there will not be
a second. If God is first, everything else will fall into place.
We're in the wrong frame of mind if we're trying so hard
to please other people that we're not seeking God first.
It's a sign that we're operating in the arm of the flesh, not
in accordance with the Spirit. Peace is not the absence of
conflict or busyness; peace is the presence of a person,
and his name is Jesus. If you want peace in your life, seek a
relationship with Jesus.

ENGAGING HEAVEN

*Are you frazzled and overwhelmed this Christmas season,
or is Jesus filling your heart with peace?*

Effective Prayers

Confess your trespasses to one another,
and pray for one another, that you may be healed.
The effective, fervent prayer of a righteous man avails much.
JAMES 5:16 NKJV

Relationship with God is not a sprint. It's daily walking with
him. That's the key to a powerful relationship and to the
righteousness required for effective and fervent prayers.
See, as we walk with God, he fills us with the confidence
and courage to know what to pray for. As we look over
the pattern of Jesus' life, we see that whenever he prayed,
miracles happened. Things in the physical were shaken when
he prayed to God in heaven. Most of us aren't awakened to
our assignment to pray because, if life starts slipping, prayer
is one of the first things we forgo. But our prayer lives matter.
True prayer is simply connecting with God and learning
to hear his voice. God desires more communion and more
connection with you. So, instead of bringing your problems
to your neighbor or friend or husband, go to God first. Watch
how prayer changes things in the physical world and how
your life is transformed.

ENGAGING HEAVEN

*Does God's voice seem clouded or absent to you?
Are you taking time to connect and commune with him?*

Two Kingdoms

Set your mind on things above,
not on things on the earth.
COLOSSIANS 3:2 NKJV

God is looking for a generation of people who will focus on him above the fray. There are two kingdoms at work every single day: the kingdom of God and the kingdom of darkness. You are going to reflect the kingdom you're most aware of, and when trials come, it's easy to recognize which kingdom that is. When issues and persecutions come, they uncover which kingdom you have been investing your time and affection in. So, when disappointments and unexpected trials happen to you, the answer is kingdom of God. When persecution comes, the answer is kingdom of God. And just the same, when distractions come, the answer is kingdom of God. Focus on the only kingdom that offers you true love and everlasting life.

ENGAGING HEAVEN

What are some of the "things of the earth," the things of the kingdom of darkness, that distract you from the kingdom of God?

Lay Them Down

Little children, guard yourselves
from worshiping anything but him.
1 John 5:21 TPT

What is considered an idol in our modern world? Well, an idol is no different now than what it has always been: it's anything that takes away from Christ's place in our lives. We bare the image of Christ, but we will begin to reflect and resemble whatever it is we're gazing at. Are we tarnishing the image of Christ he has placed on us by giving our time and attention to idols? Do we worship the Creator or his creations? We are supposed to lay the idols down; that's how God has called us to live. So today, what are we reflecting? Are we asking God what those things are for each of us? Because if we're not taking those measures and actively submitting our hearts and desires to him, other things will try to steal our attention away. Then how will we know where we stand? None of this is about condemning ourselves; it's about living so in love with God that we don't want anything more than we want him.

ENGAGING HEAVEN

Make it a point today to consume yourself with the things of God!

Maintenance of Love

Now it's time to be made new by every revelation
that's been given to you.
EPHESIANS 4:23 TPT

Everything requires maintenance. Everything. We can have the relationship we've always desired with God, but it's going to require maintenance. Let's analyze the relationships in our life. Do we become frustrated if we're asked to repeat ourselves? Has sarcasm crept into our vocabulary? Are we harboring a "look out for number one" attitude instead of a servant's heart? Do we feel the need to always prove we're right? Wise people know that, in relationships, sometimes they should give up the idea of proving they're right so they can maintain peace and unity long term. Love is worth the maintenance, and it's worth fighting for. There are relationships that we need to fight for, such as our relationship with God and with our family. There may also be a friend or a coworker or a neighbor whose relationship is worth the work of maintaining. Nothing just happens. A house doesn't fix itself, a car doesn't fix itself, and a relationship doesn't just fix itself. They all require work.

ENGAGING HEAVEN

How do you maintain love in your relationships?

Closed Minds

Don't make him angry by hardening your hearts,
like your ancestors did during the days of their rebellion,
when they were tested in the wilderness.

HEBREWS 3:8 TPT

When we don't adjust our thinking to account for the power
God has put in us, we resort to a defeated mindset. We live
inferior, not superior. We act as if we don't have any power,
as if we are unable to overcome whatever obstacle we are
facing. Closed minds and closed hearts rebel against the
things God wants to do. But a renewed mind willing to stay
open to the stirrings of the Spirit prove the will of God and
witness it come to pass. Open hearts break off the lies of the
devil. The enemy's lie is that we're hopeless, helpless, and all
alone. We start sinking into despair without realizing God's
outstretched hand. See, God already paid for everything on
the cross, and he doesn't want us to live without anything
he has already paid for. He wants us to have it all. All joy, all
forgiveness, all love, and all acceptance are available to us—
and we're never alone.

ENGAGING HEAVEN

*What does it mean to keep an open mind when facing a
situation that doesn't seem to present any good outcome?*

New Year's Resolve

God has proved his love by giving us his greatest treasure,
the gift of his Son. And since God freely offered him up
as the sacrifice for us all, he certainly won't withhold
from us anything else he has to give.

ROMANS 8:32 TPT

Resolve this year to grow your faith and go deeper with God than you've ever ventured before. It's not going to happen by accident. God has given us everything. Do you have peace in your life? Do you have love and grace and forgiveness? People go to Jesus because they're broken and in need of a Savior, and his response is to freely give them all the things they need. Do you need patience with your kids? Do you need grace for your family? Do you just need some time for yourself? Moms, especially, can lose themselves by accepting too much responsibility. What do you need from God today? What do you believe for him? Perhaps you're looking at your life and thinking there's so much you'd change. Well then, resolve to change it. God will equip you with the tools you need if you yield everything to him. This isn't a fad; it is a commitment. It's a resolve.

ENGAGING HEAVEN

What are you believing in this year? What have you written down? You need to dream. You need to believe.